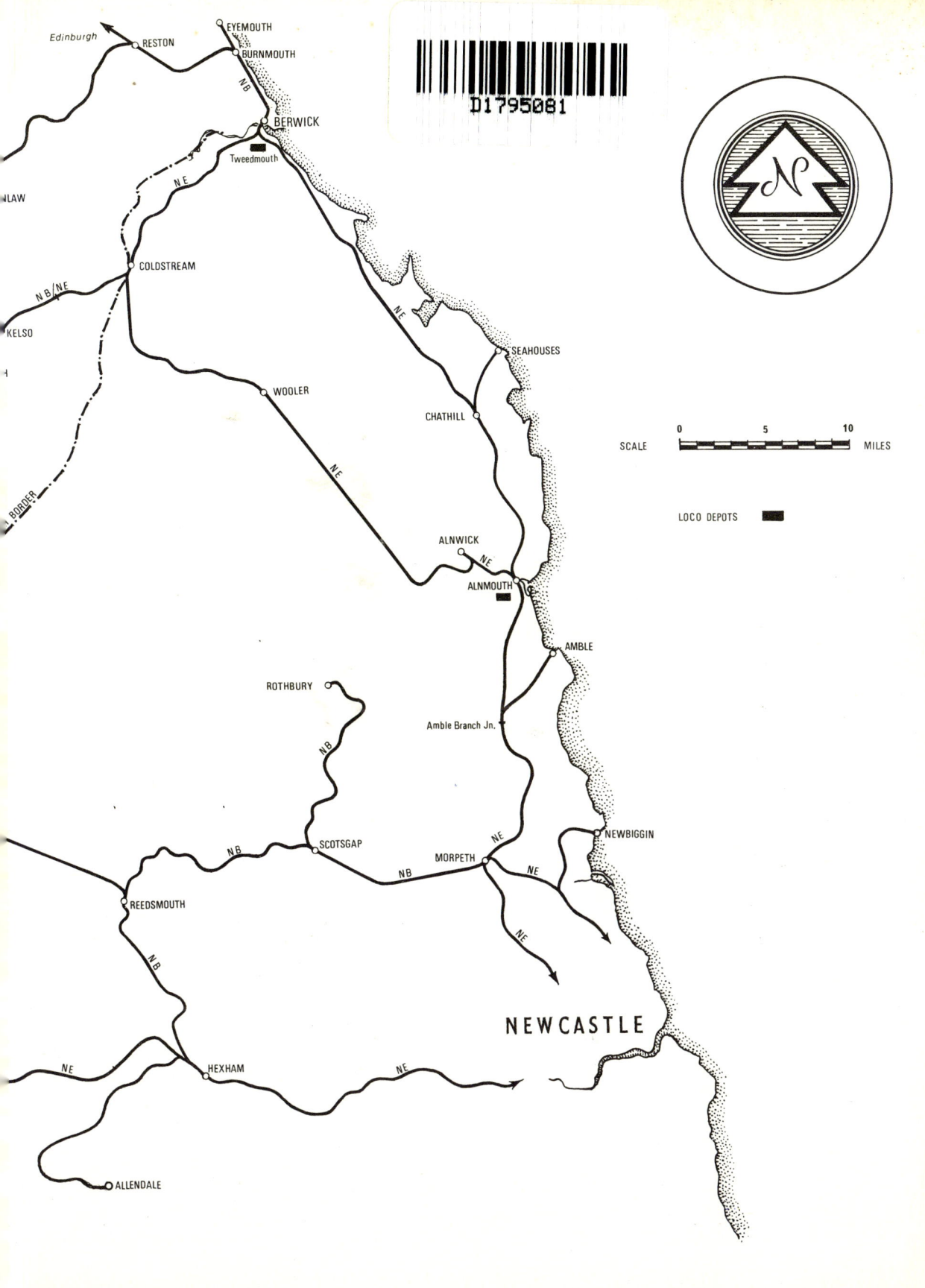

Edinburgh

RESTON

EYEMOUTH

BURNMOUTH

NB

BERWICK

Tweedmouth

NE

NLAW

NE

COLDSTREAM

NB/NE

KELSO

H

NE

WOOLER

NE

SEAHOUSES

CHATHILL

BORDER

ALNWICK

NE

ALNMOUTH

AMBLE

ROTHBURY

NB

Amble Branch Jn.

NB

SCOTSGAP

NE

NEWBIGGIN

NB

MORPETH

NB

NE

REEDSMOUTH

NE

NB

NEWCASTLE

NE

HEXHAM

NE

ALLENDALE

SCALE

0   5   10

MILES

LOCO DEPOTS

BORDER COUNTRY
BRANCH LINE
ALBUM

BORDER COUNTRY
BRANCH LINE
ALBUM

NEIL CAPLAN

LONDON
IAN ALLAN LTD

Contents

This album is dedicated to the perception, skill and enthusiasm of railway photographers — and to their so-patient wives.

First published 1981
Reprinted 1985

ISBN 0 7110 1086 2

Published by Ian Allan Ltd, Shepperton, Surrey; and printed by Ian Allan Printing Ltd at their works at Coombelands in Runnymede, England

Introduction

There is so much of grandeur in the Scottish landscape and in the Scottish railway scene: the magnificent sweep of the Firth of Forth and the great cantilevers of the Forth Bridge, the massed Grampians and the dramatic summit of Druimuachdar at 1,484ft, the bleak beauty of Sutherland and Caithness and the coiling route of the Highland line to Thurso and Wick. It is a different landscape in the Border Country of Southern Scotland and Northern England with beauty in plenty but with little of such grandeur except in the Cheviots and Liddesdale. This difference applied also to the railway scene, but the Border Country railways were full of interest and blended so well into this countryside that it is hard indeed today to grasp that what we see on the railways map as that *great empty space* of the Border Country once contained a great many branch lines.

The aim of this Album is to help in recapturing a railway system and a railway scene now lost for ever. Even a world energy crisis cannot be counted on to bring back lines such as these were. Many railway photographers regret now their pre-occupation with the main line scene because there are so few photogaphs of a number of these branches in full operation. But there is here a large and varied collection and the purpose of this Introduction is simply to help the *viewer* to set this vivid photographic record in its geographical and historical context.

The term *Border Country* is used deliberately because these branches were locked into a railway system which stretched across much of Southern Scotland and Northern England. In railway terms, the Border Country was bounded to the east by the East Coast Route; to the west by the Caledonian Railway's trunk route to Carlisle; to the south by the Newcastle & Carlisle Railway. The northern bounds are less easy to define and I admit that my choice here is a little arbitrary: a line taken from Carstairs eastwards through Dolphinton and Leadburn to Reston and the coastline. But it would be absurd to attempt to bring Edinburgh and the Lothians within the Border Country!

This forms a large area in geographical terms, but it was always an area lacking large towns and any substantial concentration of heavy industry — economic and social characteristics which certainly left their marks on the railway scene itself.

In chronological terms, the broad pattern of railway development was straightforward. The Newcastle & Carlisle Railway was opened in 1839 and the Caledonian's line to Carlisle in 1848. The North British line from Edinburgh to Berwick-upon-Tweed was completed in 1844, but the link with Newcastle-upon-Tyne was not opened until 1850. The famous and much-loved Waverley Line was opened in 1849 but only to Hawick and the extension to Carlisle by the Border Union Railway was not opened until 1862.

This was the framework within which the Border Country branch lines came to be developed. And it was the North British Railway which came to dominate the scene in spite of its own somewhat unpromising early years and the ambitions of powerful rivals. This is not the place to rehearse the often turbulent and exciting railway politics of Scotland and Northern England, except to note that from early on the North British was set on winning the lion's share. The North British almost always got its own hand quickly into the affairs of the many small, local railway companies which were promoted to construct branch lines. In most cases, it did not take long for the North British to secure the absorption of these companies into its own system. In passing, it should be noted that the criticism which came — with hindsight — to be levelled against the major railway companies for having built so many uneconomic branches, was often misdirected because it failed to allow for the intense local patriotism and pressure which prompted the first schemes for many lines.

The Border Counties Railway which was incorporated in 1854 began as a plan to link Hexham directly with Hawick via the North Tyne valley to Falstone and beyond, but later this was amended to make the link via the Border Union line at Riccarton. By 1860, the North British had effectively absorbed the Border Counties Railway whose line did not reach Riccarton until 1862. At much the same time, the North British succeeded in acquiring the Wansbeck Valley Railway which had been authorised in 1859 to link Reedsmouth with Morpeth and the Blyth & Tyne Railway. The plan of the Northumberland Central Railway in 1863 was to build a 50-mile line from Scotsgap on the Wansbeck Valley to Kelso, but this was dropped in 1867 and only the 13 miles to Rothbury were built and opened in 1870. The North British absorbed the Northumberland Central in 1872, but failed to gain control of the Blyth & Tyne Railway.

The Berwickshire Railway was incorporated in 1862 to build a line from St Boswells to Duns. By 1870, two of its five board members were North British nominees and it was vested in the North British in 1876. The Peebles Railway was authorised in 1853, opened in 1855, leased to the North British in 1861 and absorbed in 1876 (the North British opened the extension from Peebles to Galashiels in 1864).

Though the Caledonian Railway had crossed the Border with its own main line to Carlisle and with the line from Annan across the Solway viaduct, it was the North British which pursued deliberately an expansionary policy into Northern England. With control of the Border Counties, the Wansbeck Valley and the Northumberland Central Railways, the North British had built up a strong position right into the home ground of the North Eastern Railway. Talks between the two companies had taken place in 1857-58, but these proved abortive and there remained deep mutual mistrust between them in spite of their working together in the operation of the East Coast Route.

It was this mistrust which influenced the North Eastern in its acquisition of the Berwick & Kelso Railway and its construction of the line from Coldstream to Wooler and Alnwick. When, in 1862, the North Eastern was able finally to absorb the Newcastle & Carlisle Railway, it put a strong constraint on any further southward drive by the North British. In exchange for running rights granted to the North British to Carlisle from the junction at Hexham of the Border Counties, the North Eastern obtained running rights over the North British main line from Berwick to Edinburgh. This was later to prove such a bitter bone of contention between the companies.

To the west, the North British was able to limit the influence of the Caledonian to the very modest foothold of its two branches: Carstairs to Dolphinton and Symington to Peebles. In 1864-65, the North British brought off its great coup by first detaching the Edinburgh & Glasgow Railway from the Caledonian *Triple Alliance* and then absorbing it. From 1865, the battle was on for the Scottish railway crown between the North British and the Caledonian and the latter had far greater matters to look to than that of seeking to open more branches in the Border Country in rivalry with the North British lines there.

By 1876 then, the North British was predominant in the railway scene of the Border Country and it set its own seal on the area until — and some would argue beyond — the railway Grouping of 1923. This was not however a *railway empire* in economic terms. The great majority of the lines were so essentially rural and agricultural in character and the famed textile industry of the Borders was a relatively modest factor in terms of freight traffic. It was the Waverley Line alone which came to have real significance beyond the area, especially after the completion in 1875-76 of the Midland Railway's own route into Carlisle when the Waverley became an integral part of a trunk route between Scotland and England.

Economic aspects apart, the North British lines of the Border Country had everything else to arouse and hold the interest and affection of railway travellers and enthusiasts: glorious country, many historic and fascinating small towns and such pleasant folk everywhere. Perhaps it was that the people of the Border Country, having withstood the long centuries of bitter conflict, could be said to have joined together many of the virtues of Scots and English alike!

Had everything — sadly, the past tense must be dominant here because it is already a number of years since the *last* of the services over these branch lines came to an end. Even the Waverley Line itself did not long survive final closure of all its feeder lines. The only railway exploration of the Border Country now possible must take the form of railway archaeology. But this tracing of the course of former lines by the remains of trackbed, embankments, cuttings, culverts, bridges, viaducts and the rest has a strong fascination of its own.

It was easy for me in the mid-1960s to do this during so many happy tramps over partly-closed or abandoned lines, especially where lines had climbed to higher ground with the contours guiding the eye to the course of the trackbed. But it was almost as easy when in 1980 I walked again over many of them because so many features remain intact. All the major bridges and viaducts stand and look sound including Leaderfoot, Shankend and Leadhills. The cuttings and embankments remain clear in most cases and not all platforms or signalboxes have been razed. Always, there is the large reward of being in such unspoiled countryside. It is with this in mind that the album includes a good many photographs of this archaeological character — more perhaps than would be apt in a book dealing with an area which had retained a significant part of the former railway system. I hope that this feature will be helpful particularly to local historians and ramblers in the Border Country.

It is fast becoming folklore that it was the dreaded 'Beeching Axe' which cut down the branch lines which until then had been allowed to remain for the delight of railway fanatics. The reality is that withdrawal of passenger services, or even complete closure, had begun and gathered pace long before Dr Beeching (as he then was) came on the BR scene. After losing its passenger service in October 1923, the Brampton Town branch from Brampton Junction on the Newcastle & Carlisle was closed entirely at the start of 1924. In 1930, passenger services were withdrawn from both the Coldstream-Wooler-Alnwick and the Hexham-Allendale branches: a full half-century ago! Other passenger services to go in the 1930s were: Fountainhall-Lauder (1932), Leadburn-Dolphinton (complete closure 1933) and Elvanfoot-Wanlockhead (complete closure 1939).

After World War II, there were many more closures including some which came about by accident and not through a closure policy as such. These were the casualties of the famous and disastrous East Coast floods which swept across the Border Country from Liddesdale to the coast on 12 August 1948. The former Berwickshire Railway was cut at Langton Burn and the passenger service between St Boswells and Duns was never restored (that between Reston and Duns was re-opened after repairs, but survived only until 1951). At the same time the charming little branch from Roxburgh to Jedburgh was damaged and the passenger service was not restored. Taking the Border Country as a whole, as many as 60 of its stations had already lost their passenger services by the end of 1952.

The former Border Counties Railway from that truly remote junction at Riccarton, through the wild country of

Above: 'Across the Border' — the border sign at Marshall Meadows, near Berwick-upon-Tweed. *I. S. Carr*

the Cheviots and by the flashing waters of the North Tyne on to Hexham, was closed to passenger traffic in October 1956 — a little short of a century from its opening. The marvel must be that the 42-mile line had lasted so long for this was largely a remote countryside with no real prospect of ever generating large traffics. Here my thoughts are drawn back to a glowing June day in 1954 when I travelled from Hexham on the 11.10 Newcastle to Hawick, headed by 'Hunt' Class D49/2 4-4-0 No 62771 *The Rufford*. That same day, at Hawick, there were more 'D49s' including Nos 62709 *Berwickshire* and 62715 *Roxburghshire*, as well as some of the classic 'Scott' Class D30s, including Nos 62423 *Dugald Dalgetty* and 62430 *Dominie Sampson*.

These Border Country branches were never meant for impatient people intent on rushing about from place to place. They were for the patient and sociable to savour and enjoy. At stations and halts, there was time for the news of the day. Journey times were what is best described as modest, even allowing for stiff gradient work in some cases. For example, in 1910, the 25 miles from Reedsmouth to Morpeth were allowed at least 67min and the 11.05 train had 89min. The $30\frac{3}{4}$ miles from St Boswells to Reston had up to 110min and about 40min were allowed for the 10 miles from Kelso to Jedburgh via Roxburgh. But it would be unjust here to ignore the

splendid work of railwaymen and their engines tackling the heavy gradients of the Waverley Line about which Cecil J. Allen has written with such admiration. In 1905, the 09.30 Edinburgh-St Pancras was allowed only 135min for the 98.2 miles to Carlisle, with that great climb of over eight miles at 1 in 70 to Whitrope summit. Winter working on the Waverley and many other lines often presented a severe challenge.

Modest though most of the Border Country branches were, there was much fine civil engineering built into them. This applied above all to the numerous notable bridges and viaducts. It is in tribute to these engineering achievements that I have included here many illustrations of these structures. Just how well these men designed and built is best understood when one comes across their bridges and viaducts standing firmly a generation and more after abandonment of the lines.

We are accustomed now to the high speed lines with their very few intermediate stations — necessary, but so dull. The stations of the Border Country were numerous indeed — there were 14 intermediate stations between Hexham and Riccarton Junction alone. So many of the stations were really well-built of stone and were maintained attractively even during the years of decline and threatened closure. Station gardening standards were often high indeed. There is even now one happy feature of the former stations for some of these have become homes and there have been some skilful and sympathetic conversions.

There were some intriguing station names — a favourite of mine was Lamancha on the Leadburn-

Dolphinton branch, and perhaps this name appealed also to John Buchan (Lord Tweedsmuir) for he named one of his characters Lord Lamancha. Buchan truly loved the Border Country in all its parts and in all its ways and he described it superlatively well in so many of his adventure stories. Nor did he ignore the railway scene: in his tale of the Duke of Burminster (in *The Runagates Club*), he wrote of a Border Country line with the station of Langshiels on it — an echo perhaps in his ear of Langholm and of Galashiels. Those Waverley Line stations had a good ring about them: Kershope Foot, Shankend, Stobs and Belses. On the Border Counties line, there was something aptly grim-sounding about Saughtree, Deadwater, Falstone and Tarset.

But it is high time to let the photographs tell their own fascinating story. Railway enthusiasts are easy game for a laugh over their sentimental attachment to bygone days and bygone ways, but I hope that the album will help to show how the railway was woven into the landscape and the life of the Border Country and to explain how people managed to live and move around before the motor car became ubiquitous.

Acknowledgements

Twenty three lines are represented here and the paucity of known photographs has been a limiting factor for only a very few of these. I hope that the sharing out of the 240 illustrations has not been influenced seriously by my own preferences. That the former Caledonian branches seem to have come off rather well is not the result of favouritism — it is that the Caledonian main line does not have a section to itself to match those for the Waverley Line and the Newcastle & Carlisle. The Scottish lines have a larger share, proportionately to route mileage, than the English lines which reflects the larger number of very short branch lines on the Scottish side of the Border.

Motive power has pride of place, but not to the point of under-valuing the other vital aspects of railway operation. And motive power means *steam* because the Border Country was one of the very last strongholds of the steam locomotive and indeed few of its lines saw anything of the diesels apart from shunters. The featuring of viaducts and bridges has been noted in the Introduction. More than one half of the Border Country stations are illustrated. Apart from minor overlapping at the junction stations, the sections of illustrations are self-contained.

An album on this scale could not be produced without the friendly interest and help of a great many railway photographers and over 50 throughout Britain have contributed prints. All are named below in the captions (a very few photographers are 'unknown'). The help given by the following must be mentioned because it has been so generous: J. W. Armstrong, W. A. Camwell, I. S. Carr, H. C. Casserley, W. S. Sellar and W. A. C. Smith. It has been a special pleasure however to be able to include so many examples of the excellent work of less well-known photographers. A considerable proportion of the photographs used have not been published previously.

The large and varied Ian Allan Library collection has been at my disposal and I am grateful also to David & Charles for the use of one picture from the L&GRP collection. The advice and encouragement of Michael Harris (Editor, *Railway World*) has been invaluable and J. Heyman has given me much practical help over my own photographs. For background information about the Scottish railway companies, I am indebted to the staff of BR's Scottish Region who often gave me such courteous help when these records were at Waterloo Place in Edinburgh. The work of C. R. Clinker in his mammoth *Register of Closed Stations* is gratefully acknowledged.

Whitemans Green   Neil Caplan
Sussex   1980

Border Counties Railway

Only some five miles of the 42-mile line from Hexham to Riccarton Junction were on the Scottish side of the Border, but the Border Counties epitomised so much of the railway scene of the area with its chain of 14 intermediate stations, the light traffics and the sense of remoteness. In 1865, the line became part of the North British Railway's own through route to Morpeth via the Wansbeck Valley Railway. In practical terms however it was no more than a branch line throughout its lifetime of almost a century. The passenger service was withdrawn in October 1956 and the line closed in 1958.

Above: 'Scott' Class D30/2 4-4-0 No 62422 *Caleb Balderstone* with the 16.30 for Hawick at Newcastle Central on 13 July 1950. Reid's design for the North British Railway was introduced in 1912 and the 'Scotts' were identified closely with the Border Country for almost a half-century. *L. A. Strudwick*

Below: Border Counties junction at Hexham, with the tracks curving to the left for the approach to the bridge over the North Tyne. Class K1 2-6-0 No 62026 passing under the gantry of Hexham West signalbox with a freight for Carlisle in 1950. *J. W. Armstrong*

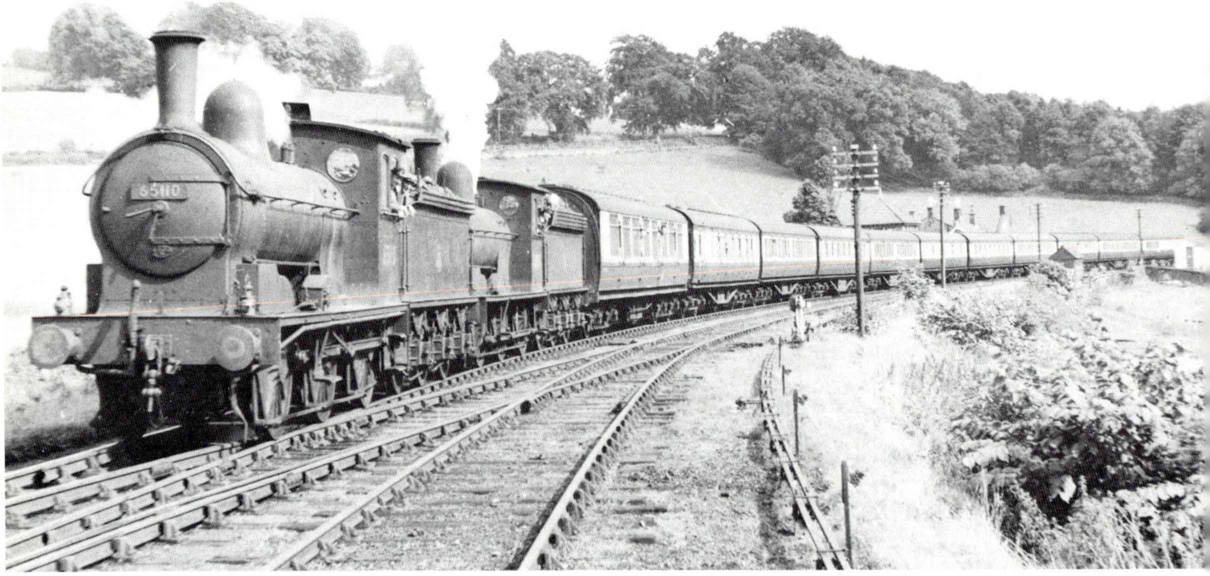
65110

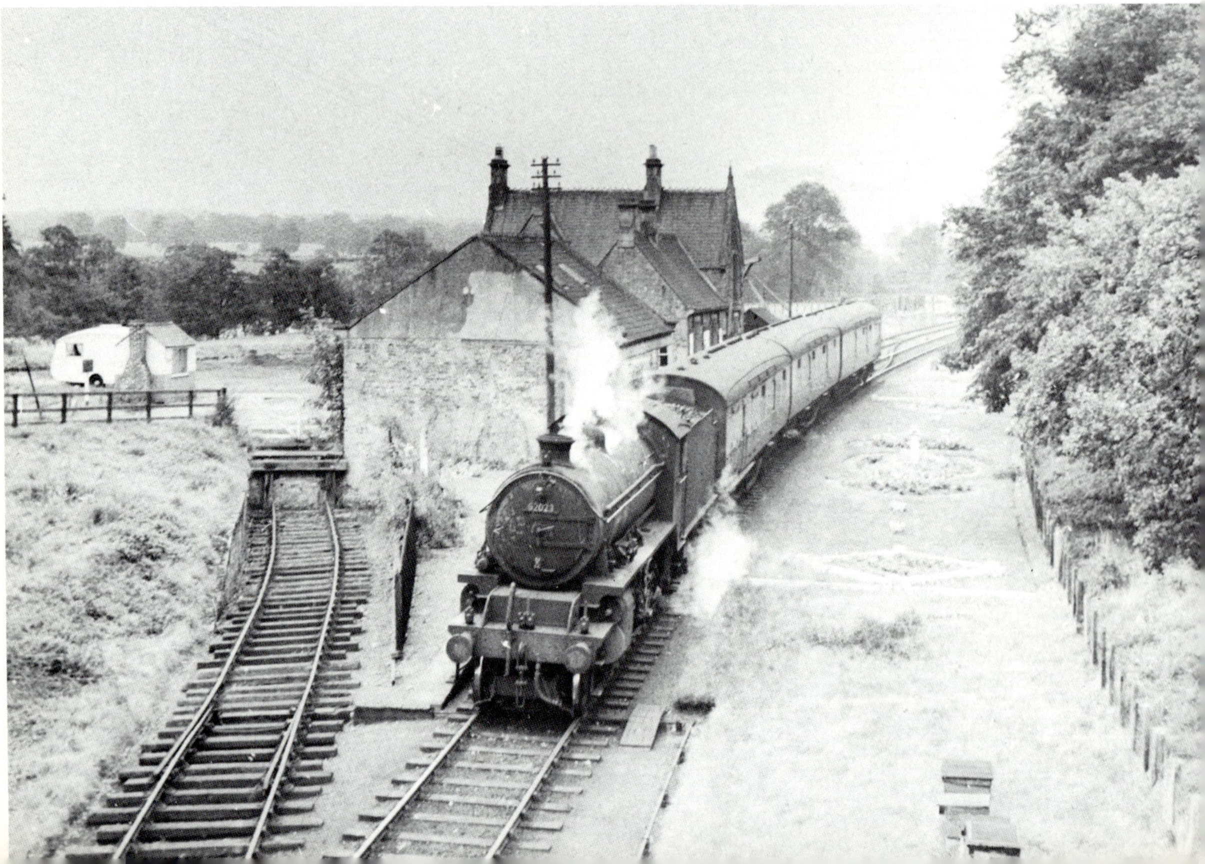

Above left: Approaching Wall station, c1952: Class J21 0-6-0 Nos 65110 and 65090 working a troop special for summer camp near Woodburn. This notable duty for the humble 'J21s' was brought about by line restrictions on the Wansbeck Valley east of Reedsmouth. A pair of 'J21's brought the specials on from Newcastle to Hexham where the pilot engine came off because double-heading was not permitted over the North Tyne bridge; the train engine then took the special forward to Wall to be joined there by the pilot running light from Hexham (I am indebted for this information to Mr J. W. Armstrong). *J. W. Armstrong*

Left: Humshaugh station on 12 October 1956: Class K1 2-6-0 No 62023 with a train for Hexham. *W. A. Camwell*

Above: At Barrasford on 12 September 1956 and the grimy condition of Class K3/2 2-6-0 No 61990 was unhappily in keeping with these last weeks of the passenger service. *I. S. Carr*

Right: Wark station on 12 October 1956: Standard 2-6-0 No 77011 with the 12.00 train from Hexham to Hawick. *W. A. Camwell*

Above: At Reedsmouth on 13 October 1956 — the eve of withdrawal of the passenger service — and Standard 2-6-0 No 77011 waits with the 08.55 Hawick-Newcastle. The Wansbeck Valley line to the right. *J. W. Armstrong*

Below: The engine shed at Reedsmouth on 7 July 1951: on shed, Class J21 0-6-0 No 65042. *W. A. Camwell*

Above: Reedsmouth on 8 May 1950: Class J39/1 0-6-0 No 64705 with the 16.30 Hexham-Hawick. *W. A. Camwell*

Below: The final scheduled passenger train over the Border Counties line: Class K1 2-6-0 No 62022 leaving Reedsmouth for Riccarton Junction on 13 October 1956. Note the 'wreath' on the smokebox door which was a tradition for last day services. *J. W. Armstrong*

Above: Class J21 0-6-0 No 65061 at Reedsmouth with the empty stock of the traditional excursion run from Tyneside via the Wansbeck Valley line to Bellingham for the Agricultural Show on 22 September 1956. Even after closure of the Border Counties line as such, excursions were run on Bellingham Show Day until 1963 when the Wansbeck Valley line was closed finally west of Woodburn. *I. S. Carr*

Left: Near Bellingham: 'Scott' Class D30/2 4-4-0 No 62425 *Ellangowan* with a Hawick-Newcastle train on 20 September 1952. *J. W. Armstrong*

Above right: Tarset station on 13 October 1956: a Class V3 2-6-2T with a train for Hexham. *J. W. Armstrong*

Right: Thorneyburn station on 12 October 1956: Standard 2-6-0 No 77011 with a Hexham-Hawick train. *W. A. Camwell*

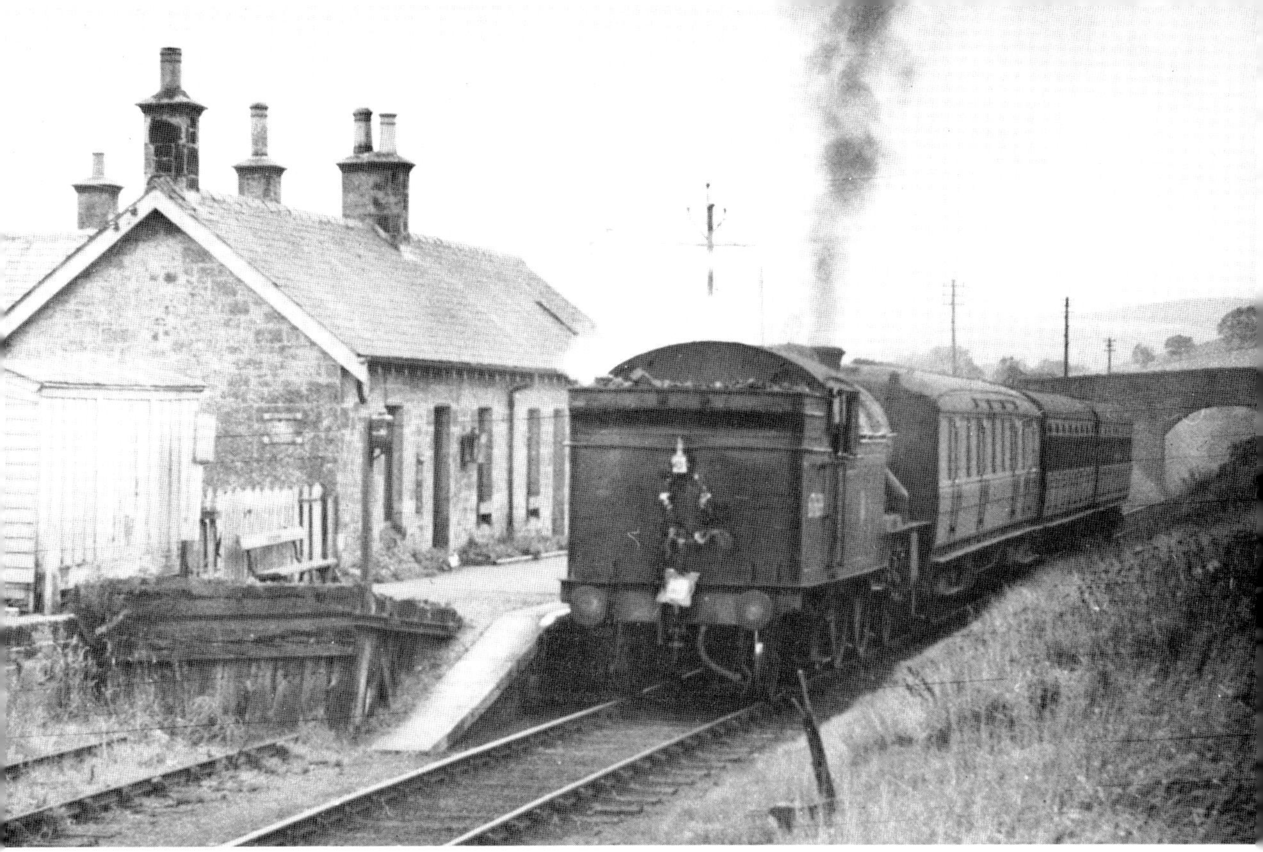

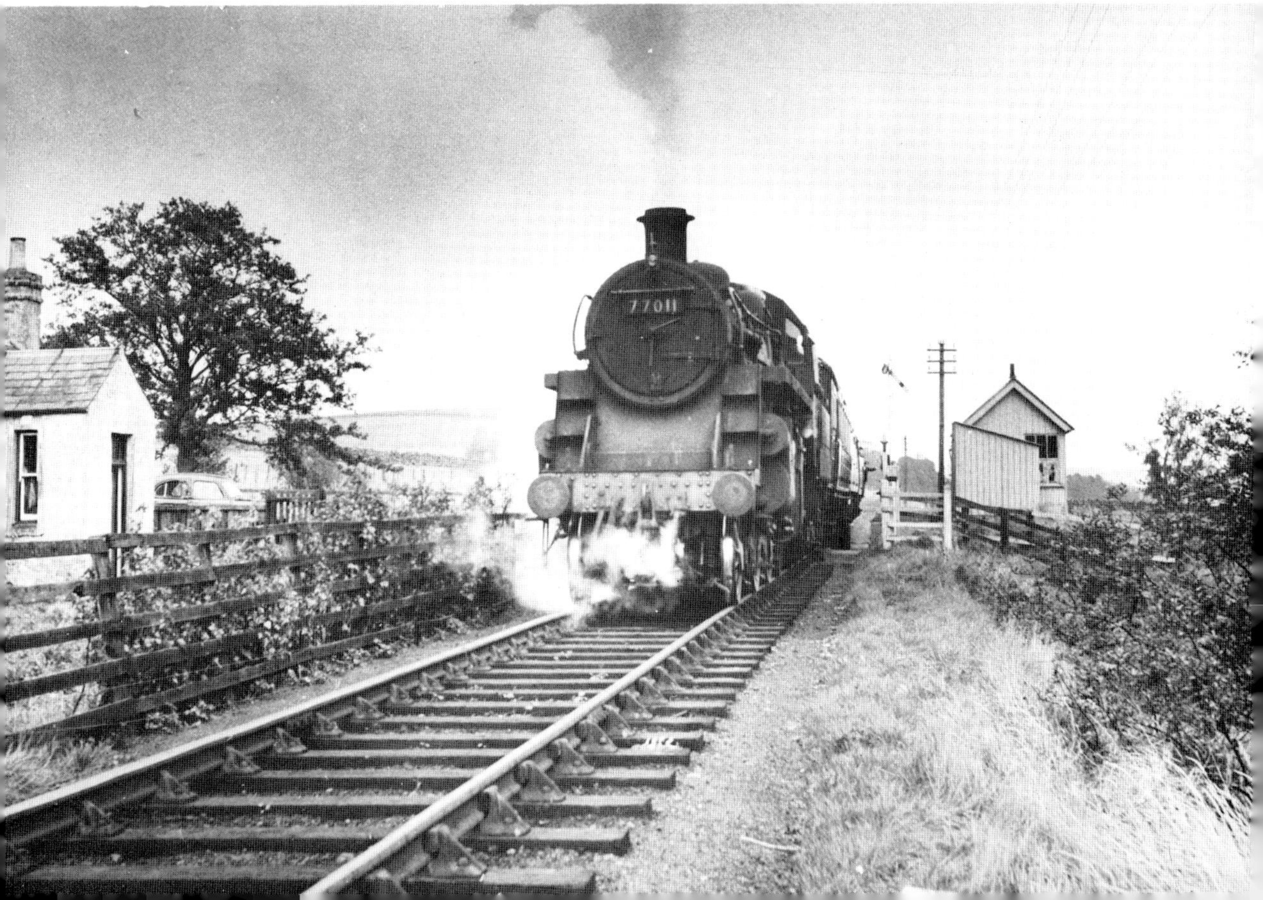
77011

Above: Plashetts station on 13 October 1956.
J. W. Armstrong

Below: Kielder Forest station in October 1956: Standard 2-6-0 No 77011 with the 11.20 Newcastle-Hawick passing Class V3 2-6-2T with the 13.40 (SO) Kielder-Hexham.
J. W. Armstrong

Above: At Kielder Forest on 15 September 1956: Class V3 2-6-2T No 67687 with the 13.40 (SO) to Hexham. Note in the background the dark mass of the forest itself — it never generated the freight traffic which once had been hoped. *J. W. Armstrong*

Below: Near the Border itself on 17 July 1955: Standard 2-6-0 No 76049 with a Ramblers' Special of eight coaches. *J. D. Smith*

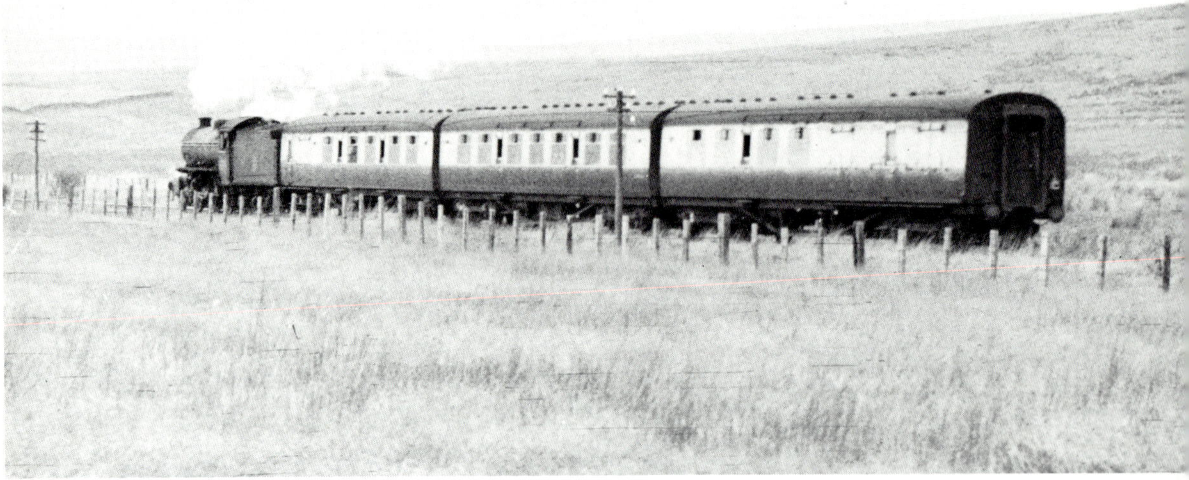

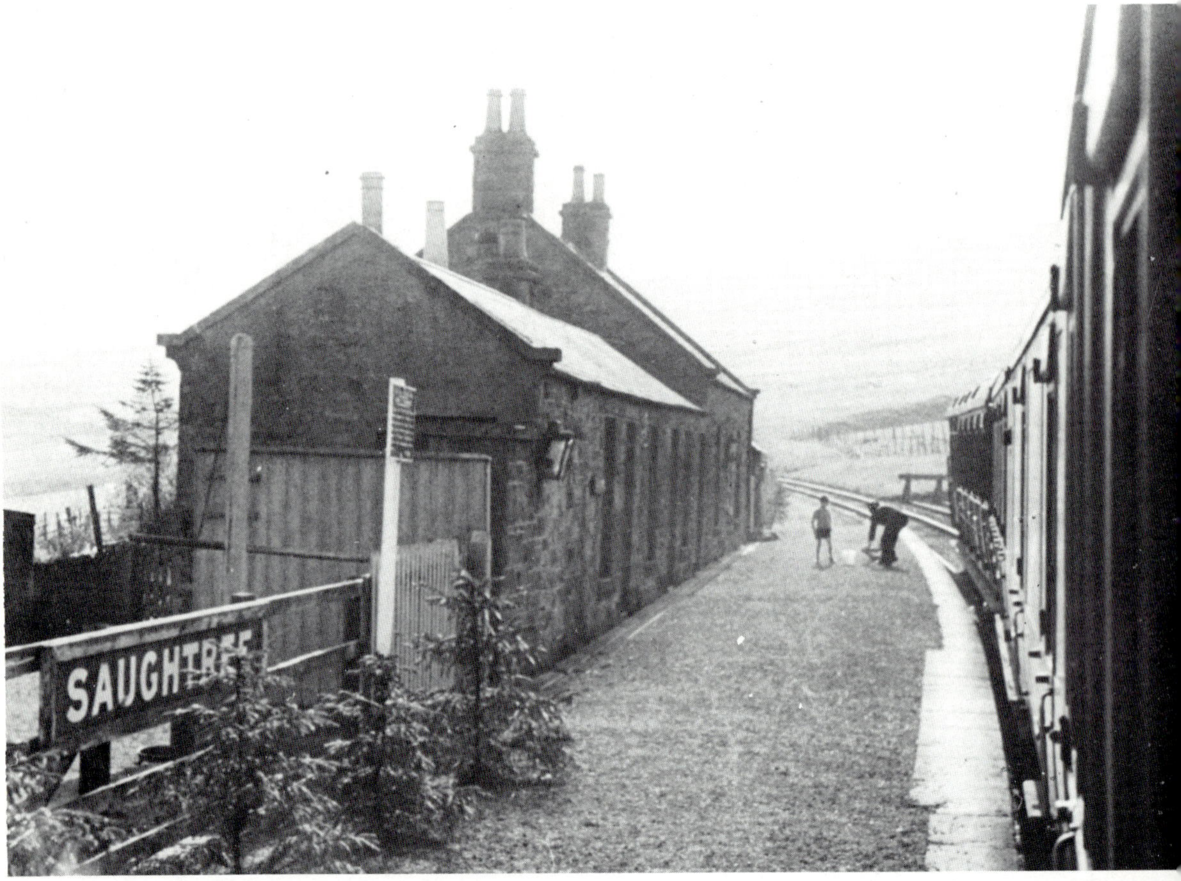
SAUGHTREE

Above left: On the Border between Deadwater and Saughtree: Class K1 2-6-0 No 62022 with a train for Hawick. This was in the last days of the passenger service in October 1956. *J. W. Armstrong*

Below left: Saughtree station on 28 April 1952 — by this time, Saughtree was being served by only one passenger train in each direction on three days a week. *H. C. Casserley*

Above: The former station at Saughtree on 4 August 1964 in all its bleak isolation. *N. Caplan*

Below: The junction set 'in the middle of nowhere': Riccarton Junction in July 1952. The Waverley Line tracks swinging off to the left and up on the right the railway staff cottages. *Ian Allan Library*

Above: The engine shed at Riccarton Junction on 19 June 1949: on shed, 'Scott' Class D30/2 4-4-0 No 62432 *Quentin Durward.* *W. A. Camwell*

Below: Riccarton Junction in 1952: Standard 2-6-0 No 76046 with a train for Newcastle. Note the grocery shop of the Hawick Co-operative Society on the station platform — a vital service indeed for the so-isolated railway community of Riccarton. *N. K. Ham*

Wansbeck Valley Railway

Above: Class J21 0-6-0 No 65042 waiting at Reedsmouth on 7 July 1951 with the one-coach 07.44 for Scotsgap. In the background 'Hunt' Class D49/2 4-4-0 No 62771 *The Rufford* with the 06.47 Riccarton Junction-Hexham. *W. A. Camwell*

Below: Woodburn station on 7 July 1951: No 65042 with a Scotsgap-Reedsmouth train. Note the beautifully kept station and garden. *W. A. Camwell*

The 25-mile line from Reedsmouth to Morpeth remained a local line dominated by mineral traffic. It might have been a different story if the North British had succeeded in taking over the Blyth & Tyne Railway and thus had reached through to Tyneside at its own hand. Even in 1914, the passenger service was limited to only three trains in each direction on weekdays. The service was withdrawn in September 1952. The freight service continued over the line through to Reedsmouth until November 1963 after which it terminated at Woodburn until final closure came in October 1966. Apart from 'last day' scenes, photographs of the passenger service in operation have proved elusive but — once again — Mr W. A. Camwell has come to the rescue.

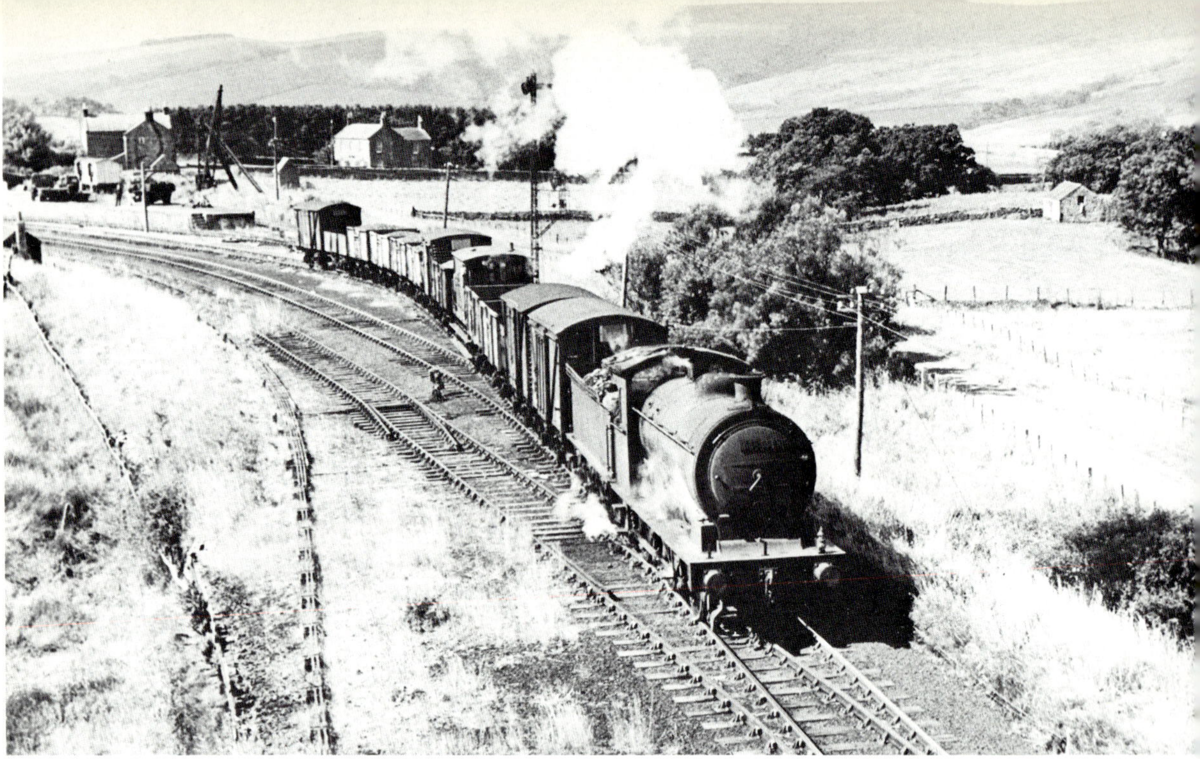

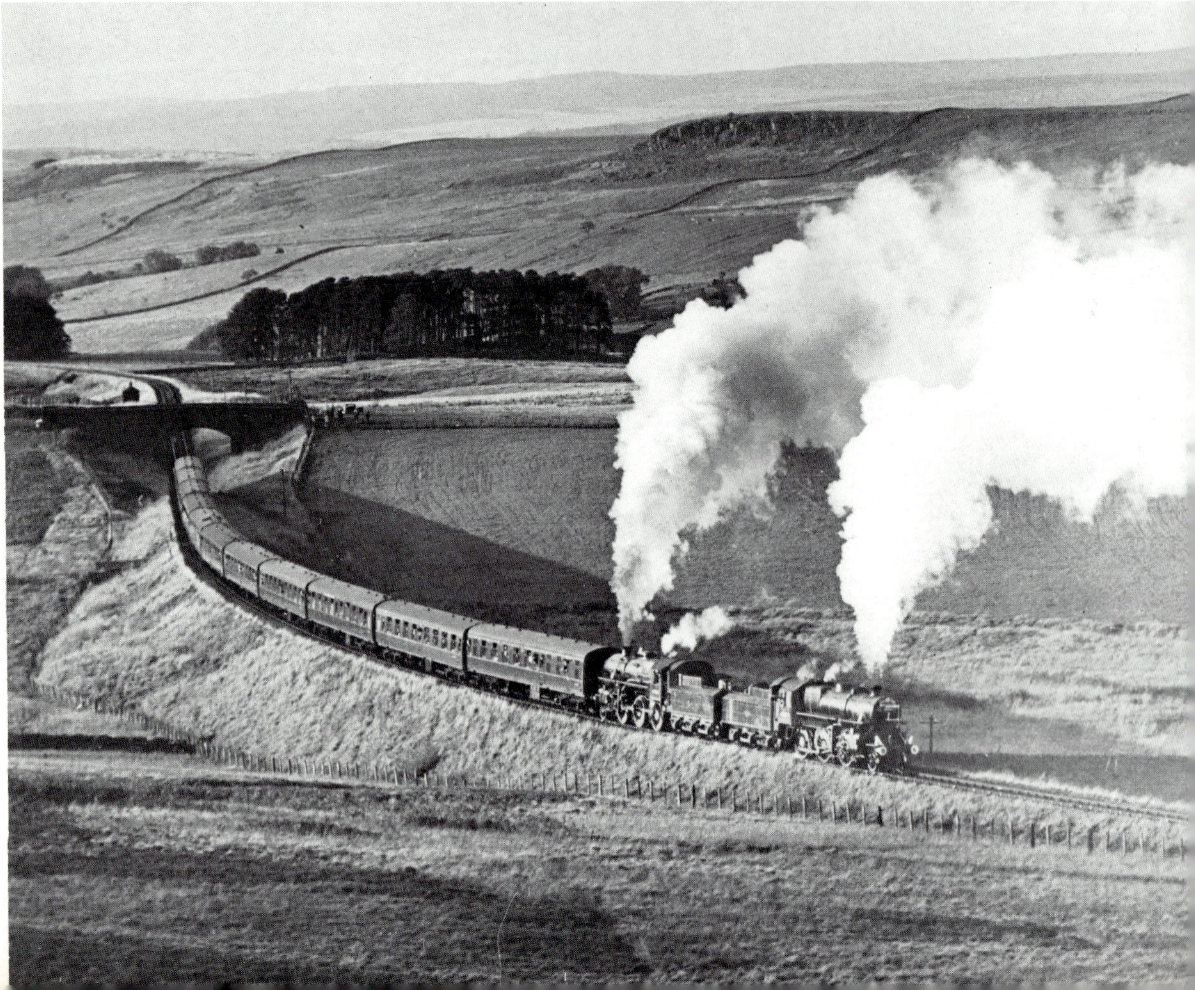

Above left: Class J27 0-6-0 No 65855 shunting Woodburn yard on 25 August 1966 before working the weekly branch freight to Morpeth. *G. McLean*

Below left: An impressive sight for the Wansbeck Valley: a pair of Ivatt 2-6-0s Nos 43000 and 43063 with 11 coaches up climbing the 1 in 62 out of Woodburn on 2 October 1966. This was the 'Wansbeck Piper' excursion organised by Gosforth Round Table to mark final closure of the line from 3 October — the last weekly freight had worked from Woodburn to Morpeth on 29 September. *M. S. Burns*

Above: Knowesgate station on 20 September 1952: the train passing through was an excursion run after withdrawal of the scheduled passenger service from 15 September 1952. *J. W. Armstrong*

Below: Scotsgap station on 7 July 1951: Class J21 0-6-0 No 65042 with the 10.46 for Reedsmouth. Note the very clear old-style station name-board describing correctly 'Scotsgap Jct' — for the Rothbury branch. *W. A. Camwell*

Top left: Scotsgap station on
13 September 1952: Class J21 0-6-0
No 65042 with a train from
Reedsmouth for Morpeth and
Class G5 0-4-4T No 67341 with the
Rothbury train. *J. W. Armstrong*

Centre left: Taking water at Scotsgap
on 23 June 1966: Class J27 0-6-0
No 65814 with the weekly freight from
Morpeth to Woodburn.
R. E. B. Siviter

Bottom left: The humble little station
at Middleton on 13 September 1952.
J. W. Armstrong

Right: Near Angerton on
22 September 1966: Class J27 0-6-0
No 65842 with the branch freight and
looking in fine trim — as well it might
after the attention it had received at
the hands of a band of railway
photographers drawn to Woodburn on
the eve of final closure of the line!
D. E. Gouldthorp

Below: Angerton station on 28 July
1966: Class J27 0-6-0 No 65860 with
the weekly Morpeth-Woodburn
freight. *L. Sandler*

Northumberland Central Railway

The 13-mile branch from Scotsgap Junction to Rothbury was opened as late as November 1870 — a small part only of the original scheme to construct a line north to reach Kelso. In North British days, there was a substantial mineral traffic of coal and stone. There were then four sidings under Fontburn, including the Whitehouse siding for the Ewesley Quarry Company and the Font siding for Tynemouth Corporation's reservoir nearby. The branch lost its passenger service in September 1952 when the Wansbeck Valley service was withdrawn and final closure came in November 1963.

Above left: At the junction station on 13 September 1952: Class J21 0-6-0 No 65042 suitably 'wreathed' ready for this last day of passenger services over the Northumberland Central and Wansbeck Valley lines. *J. W. Armstrong*

Below left: Class J21 0-6-0 No 65035 arriving at Scotsgap on 7 July 1951 with a freight from Rothbury for Morpeth. *W. A. Camwell*

Above: Class J25 0-6-0 No 65727 at Scotsgap on 8 August 1958 with a Morpeth-Rothbury freight. *I. S. Carr*

Below: A typical rural branch line scene: Ewesley station on 13 September 1952 with Class G5 0-4-4T No 67341 dropping a horse box. *J. W. Armstrong*

Above: Brinkburn station on 6 July 1951: Class G5 0-4-4T
No 67296 with the 17.50 Morpeth-Rothbury.
W. A. Camwell

Below: Rothbury station on 6 July 1951: Class G5 0-4-4T
No 67296 with the 17.50 from Morpeth. Note the little
engine shed and the turntable forming part of the line into
the station platform. *W. A. Camwell*

Above: Class J21 0-6-0 No 65035 shunting Rothbury yard on 13 September 1952. The decorations marked not only the last day of passenger service but also the sad occasion of closure of the Rothbury shed. *J. W. Armstrong*

Below: Class J27 0-6-0 No 65822 shunting Rothbury yard on 25 October 1962 just before final closure of the branch. *S. C. Crook*

Berwick, Kelso & St Boswells

The acquisition of the Berwick & Kelso Railway by the North Eastern Railway was a modest counter-move to the drive into Northumberland by the North British Railway. It took North Eastern rails into Scotland — only just — because it was the North British which pushed the line eastward from Kelso to meet the North Eastern at Sprouston junction. Though the North Eastern had running rights to St Boswells, its own passenger service from Berwick-upon-Tweed operated only as far as Kelso.

This division of the line resulted in a distinctly odd passenger service. By Border Country standards, there were numerous trains over the line but with no through service between Berwick and St Boswells. The people of Kelso alone had the full benefit of the sharing of the service by the two railway companies for they had six trains in each direction both to Berwick and to St Boswells in 1914. There were also two Sunday trains to and from St Boswells. Journey times however were leisurely with 55-60min allowed for the $23\frac{1}{2}$ miles from Kelso to Berwick.

The line retained a passenger service right up until June 1964, though east of Kelso the only stations served latterly were Coldstream and Norham. A very interesting point about the service to Kelso in the 1950s was that there was a through train to Kelso from Edinburgh at 17.11 running via St Boswells which reached Kelso at 19.02. The line was closed entirely at the end of March 1965.

The Royal Border Bridge over the Tweed stands as a noble tribute to the great and varied skills of its designer, Robert Stephenson. The bridge has an overall length of 2,160ft and it was opened in 1850 by Queen Victoria.

Below: Berwick-upon-Tweed station in April 1965 — a handsome building worthy of the historic border town. *N. Caplan*

Above: Standard 2-6-0 No 78048 arriving at Berwick on 24 May 1962 with the 16.00 from St Boswells comprising just one passenger coach and several vans. *M. Mensing*

Below: Class D20/1 4-4-0 No 62387 at Berwick with an inspection saloon. *W. P. Conelly*

Above: Class K1 2-6-0 No 62002 marshalling hopper wagons at Berwick in October 1963. *N. Caplan*

Below: Standard 2-6-0 No 78048 crossing the bridge on 1 June 1962 with the 08.25 from St Boswells. *M. Mensing*

Above: Class V2 2-6-2 No 60978 marshalling empty stock on the bridge on 4 September 1962. *V. Wake*

Below: Tweedmouth shed in April 1965. Note the ramp to the right for coaling wagons. *N. Caplan*

Left: Inside Tweedmouth shed in April 1965 — with Class K1 No 62050 and Standard 2-6-0 No 77004 and, in the background, the Tweedmouth breakdown crane. *N. Caplan*

Centre left: Norham station on 20 July 1963: Standard 2-6-0 No 78049 with a train for St Boswells. Mr Peter J. Short, who was in charge of Norham at the time of closure of the line, bought the station including the station house and he has since given it loving care. Now it is a great attraction to railway enthusiasts. *J. Spencer Gilks*

Below: Class J21 0-6-0 No 65110 with an inspection saloon at Twizell in 1956. When the Berwick & Kelso Railway was first built, there was no Twizell station — Cornhill came next after Norham. *P. Ward*

Above right: Coldstream station in September 1958: Standard 2-6-0 No 78047 with a train for Berwick. *G. E. Smith*

Right: Ivatt 2-6-0 No 46482 moving on to vans at Coldstream before working a freight to Kelso on 1 June 1962. *M. Mensing*

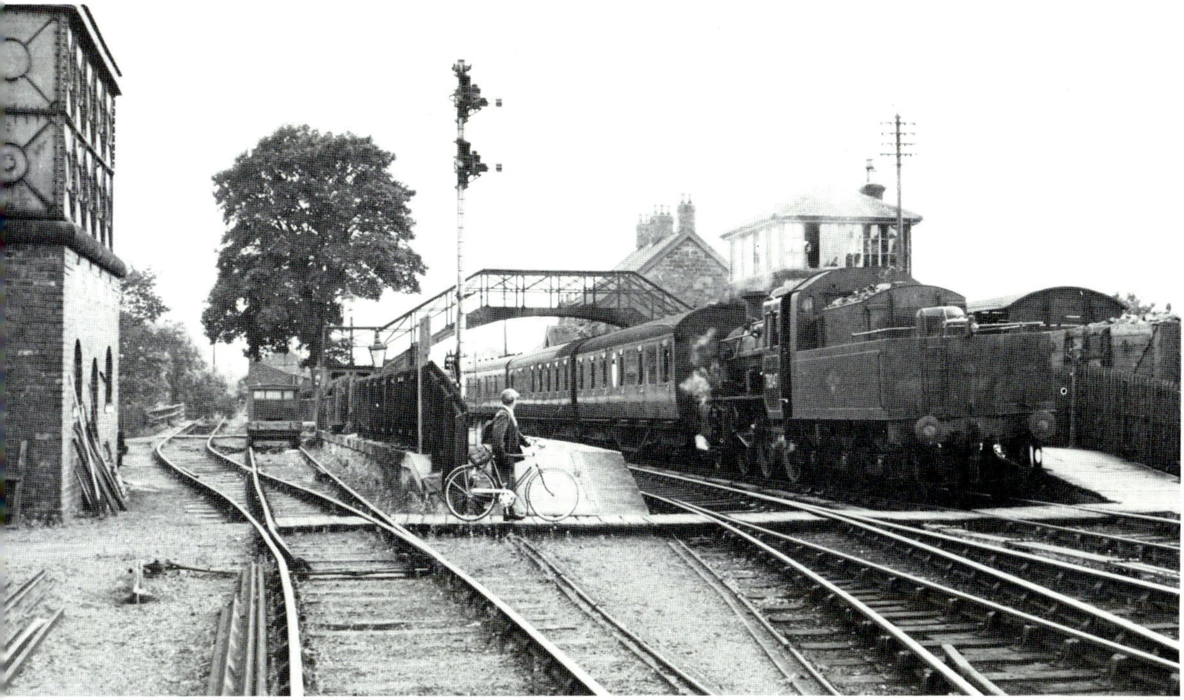

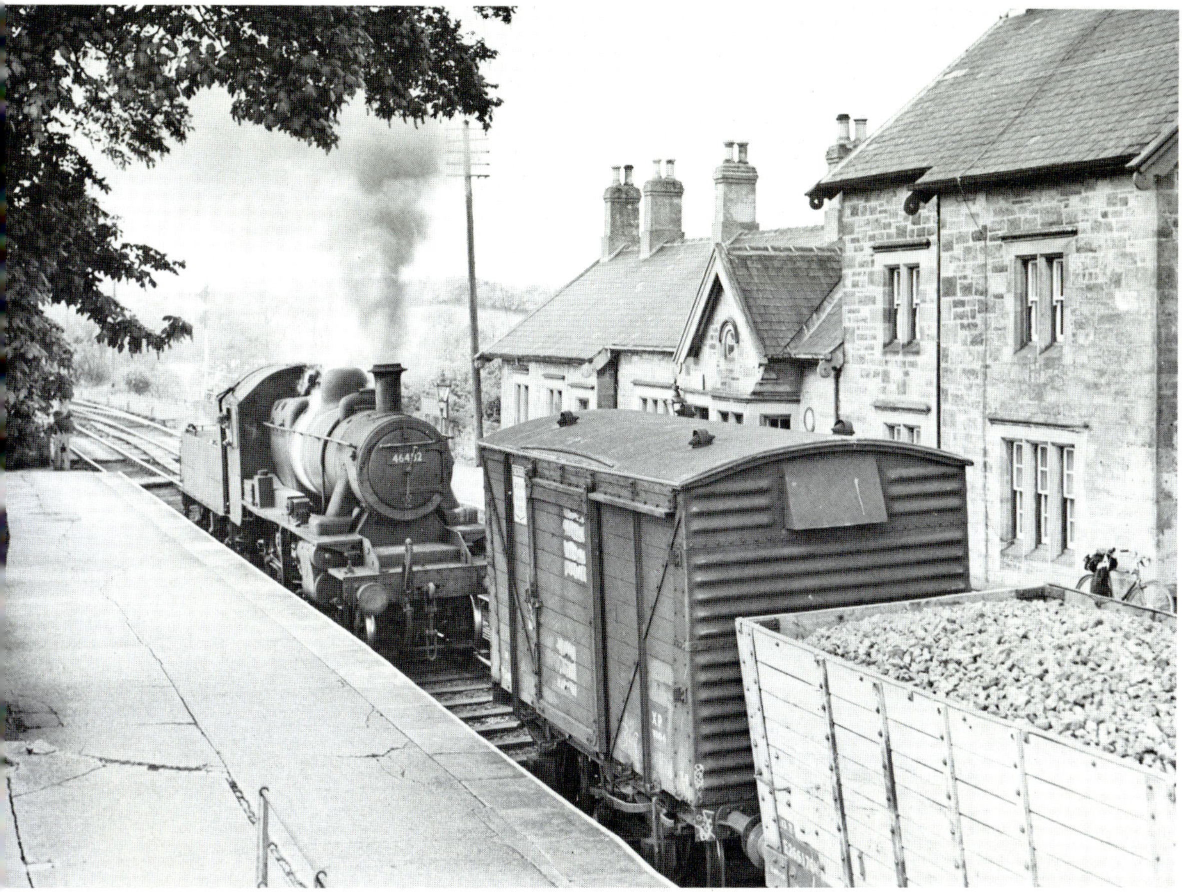

Above: Sprouston station: note the typical small engine shed to the left of the water tank. *C. J. B. Sanderson*

Below: Kelso station on 14 October 1954: 'Scott' Class D30/2 4-4-0 No 62440 *Wandering Willie* with a train for St Boswells. *W. A. Camwell*

Above: At Kelso on 20 July 1963: Standard 2-6-0 No 78049 waiting with the 11.52 (SO) to St Boswells.
J. Spencer Gilks

Below: Class V1 2-6-2T No 67659 at Kelso, setting back to attach a van to the 16.50 St Boswells-Berwick.
N. R. Knight

Above: Against the striking background of the Eildons, Standard 2-6-0 No 78049 heading the 12.00 Berwick-St Boswells towards Roxburgh in September 1962. *M. Dunnett*

Below: Roxburgh station on 18 July 1963: Ivatt 2-6-0 No 43138 waiting with a freight for Jedburgh, for the 11.42 St Boswells-Kelso (behind Standard 2-6-0 No 78049) to clear the single line. *J. Spencer Gilks*

Above: Rustic simplicity and neatness: Rutherford station in August 1964 shortly after withdrawal of the passenger service. *N. Caplan*

Below: A humble duty indeed for a 'Glen' class 4-4-0: No 62484 *Glen Lyon* leaving Maxton with a freight from Jedburgh to Galashiels on 1 August 1961. *D. E. Esau*

Above: At Maxton on 25 June 1964: Standard 2-6-0 No 78049 with a freight for St Boswells passing over the level crossing. Note the singled track. *N. Caplan*

Below: St Boswells station on 13 May 1950: 4-4-0 No 62208 with the 18.35 from Berwick. Note the old-style large station board 'Change for Jedburgh, Kelso and Berwick' — though the passenger service to Jedburgh had ceased in August 1948. *W. A. Camwell*

The Jedburgh Branch

The 7-mile line from Roxburgh was a particularly attractive one with its course close to the Teviot and its little stations set in the fields. Before World War I, the small town of Jedburgh had a good passenger service with six trains in each direction on weekdays and two trains in each direction on Sundays. The damage caused by the East Coast floods in August 1948 occasioned the immediate withdrawal of the passenger service, though the freight service was restored quite quickly and survived until 1965.

Above: Kirkbank station on 5 August 1964 — by this time reduced to the status of 'Unstaffed Public Siding'. When the branch was first opened, this station was known as Old Ormiston. *N. Caplan*

Below: At Nisbet on 29 May 1964 with a distinguished visitor indeed to the little branch: 'Jubilee' 4-6-0 No 45696 *Arethusa* working the branch freight. The Nisbet Post Office was in the station building. *J. Spencer Gilks*

Above: Jedfoot station on 5 August 1964 — first called Jed Foot and later known as Jedfoot Bridge. *N. Caplan*

Below: Jedburgh station on 21 June 1947: Class D20 4-4-0 LNER No 2358 with the 17.30 train for Kelso. The sidings and the large crane evidencing the former importance of the railway to the town. *W. A. Camwell*

Above: Standard 2-6-0 No 78049 about to leave Jedburgh for Roxburgh on 3 August 1964. *N. Caplan*

Below: The unassuming station building at Jedburgh on 3 August 1964. *N. Caplan*

Coldstream, Wooler & Alnwick

The construction of the $35\frac{1}{4}$-mile line through the Northumberland agricultural belt was governed more perhaps by railway company strategy than by conviction on the part of the North Eastern Railway that such a line would generate profitable traffics. The passenger service was always modest with four trains only in each direction on weekdays in 1914. The service was withdrawn as long ago as September 1930. The freight service continued throughout until March 1953 when the line was closed entirely southward from Wooler. Finally, the Coldstream to Wooler freight service was closed early in 1965 when the Tweed Valley line closed also. The line could well have served as an almost perfect example of the rural branches.

Above: Coldstream station in April 1962 with its really good-looking range of stone buildings. Class J39/1 0-6-0 No 64813 shunting. *P. Ward*

Above: Mindrum station on 5 August 1964 — 34 years after withdrawal of the passenger service. A substantial building with a handsome station house and many decorative touches. This was something of a standard design for the branch, as the illustrations below of Akeld and Wooler show. *N. Caplan*

Below: The miniature warehouse and yard at Mindrum. *N. Caplan*

Above: Kirknewton station on 14 April 1963: Ivatt 2-6-0 No 46474 with a special train. *W. S. Sellar*

Below: Between Kirknewton and Akeld: Ivatt 2-6-0 No 46475 with a freight for Wooler passing Yeavering Crossing on 23 February 1963. *A. Moyes*

Above: Akeld station on 28 May 1959: Ivatt 2-6-0
No 46476 running light engine. *J. Spencer Gilks*

Below: Approaching Wooler: Standard 2-6-0 No 78025
with the daily freight from Coldstream. *W. A. Camwell*

Above: Wooler station on 12 July 1955: Class J21 0-6-0
No 65099 waiting to leave for Coldstream and Berwick.
W. A. Camwell

Below: Ivatt 2-6-0 No 46476 at Wooler on 28 May 1959.
J. Spencer Gilks

Above: Ilderton station on 27 February 1953 — the eve of closure of the line south of Wooler. Class D20/2 4-4-0 No 62371 with a freight for Alnwick. *J. W. Armstrong*

Below: Hedgeley station on 27 February 1953 — again with No 62371. Note the signalman handing over the token to the driver for single-line working. *J. W. Armstrong*

Above: Whittingham station on 27 February 1953 — an outstandingly good country station laid out with an optimistic view of likely traffics. *J. W. Armstrong*

Below: The notably fine station at Alnwick in 1954 — with its fine twin roofs. Class D20/1 4-4-0 No 62381 with a train for Alnmouth. *W. A. Camwell*

Alnmouth to Alnwick

Just a little 3-mile local line even if it nominally provided a link between the central parts of Northumberland and the East Coast main line at Alnmouth. The greatest distinction enjoyed by the branch came late in life when it retained steam working until June 1966 and when it was visited by such powerful engines as the Class V2 2-6-2s and even by a Standard Class 9F 2-10-0!

Above: Alnmouth station — facing south — on 5 September 1955. *H. C. Casserley*

Right: Class K1 2-6-0 No 62011 running round its train at Alnmouth in preparation for a return trip to Alnwick on 18 June 1966. *V. Wake*

52

Left: Class V2 2-6-2 No 60836 with the 09.05 Alnmouth-Alnwick crossing the graceful viaduct over the Aln on 31 May 1966. *M. S. Burns*

Below: Class J39/2 0-6-0 No 64924 arriving at Alnwick with the 17.05 from Alnmouth on 27 May 1962. *M. Mensing*

Below left: Half-way to Alnwick: Class K1 2-6-0 No 62012 with the 11.44 from Alnmouth on 27 June 1964. *M. Dunnett*

Above: Class K1 2-6-0 No 62011 leaving Alnwick with the 17.35 for Alnmouth on 19 March 1966 — and failing conspicuously to 'consume its own smoke' as Parliament had demanded of the steam locomotive! *I. S. Carr*

Below: The branch's finest hour: Standard 9F 2-10-0 No 92099 with the 16.48 from Alnmouth on 18 June 1966. *G. McLean*

The Berwickshire Railway

The 30¾-mile line from Reston on the East Coast main line to St Boswells (42 miles from Berwick-upon-Tweed) ran through the heart of Berwickshire. It remained a quiet, rural branch though it served Duns and Greenlaw which together shared the functions of County Town. Even in 1914, there were only three trains in each direction on weekdays working through from St Boswells and Berwick though there were additional trains between Duns and Berwick and Duns and St Boswells. As noted in the Introduction, it was the damage caused by the East Coast floods of August 1948 which brought about the withdrawal of the passenger service between St Boswells and Duns and the restriction of the freight service to Greenlaw only, east of St Boswells. Final closure came in 1965.

Above: Reston station on 18 September 1950: Class G5 0-4-4T No 67248 with the 15.58 to Duns. Note the North British style station name-board 'Change Carriages for Duns'. *H. D. Bowtell*

Below: Reston station on 6 September 1955 showing the lay-out with the Berwickshire's tracks to the right and a good example of a turntable. *H. C. Casserley*

Above: Near Reston in North British days: a rebuilt Wheatley 2-4-0 No 1246 with a train for Duns from St Boswells. *L&GRP courtesy David & Charles*

Below: Duns station on 13 May 1950: Class G5 0-4-4T No 67303 with a local train from Reston. Note the engine number painted on the buffer beam and the then so-familiar advertisement for Virol — a reminder of the times when station and lineside advertising was of major importance. *W. A. Camwell*

Above: A photograph which recaptures so well the atmosphere of a Border Country station after Market Day: a cattle train about to leave Duns for Reston after Duns Cattle Fair on 18 September 1950, the train engine was Class K1 2-6-0 No 62007. *H. D. Bowtell*

Below: Duns station on 6 August 1964 and looking in good shape for a station which had lost its passenger service 13 years previously. The track had been singled. *N. Caplan*

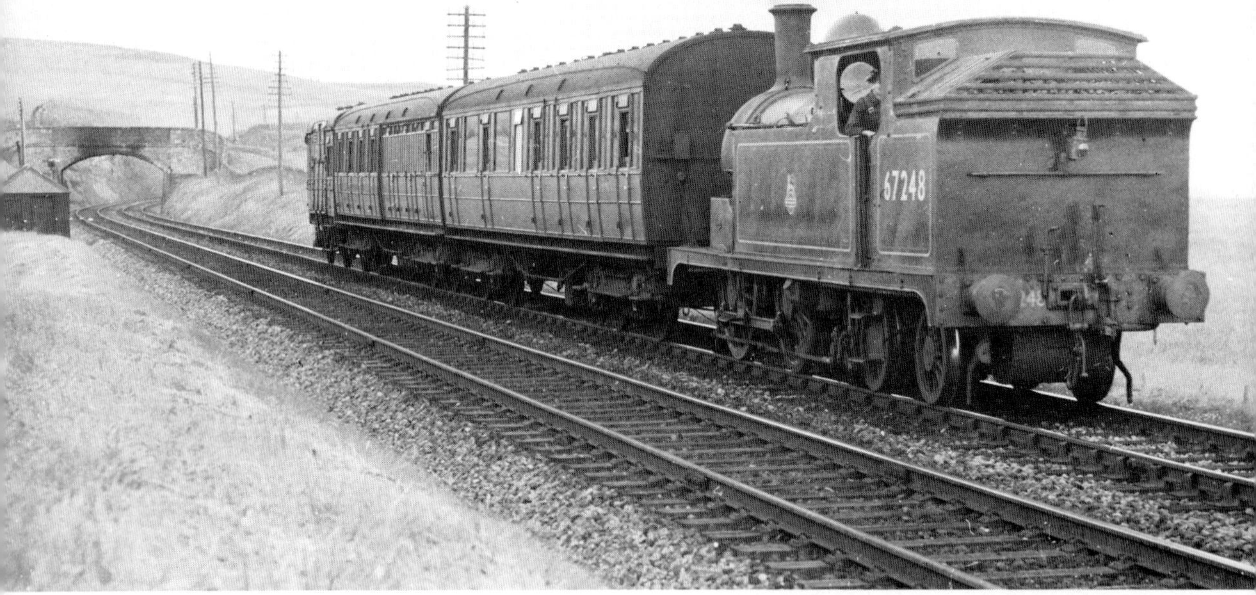
67248

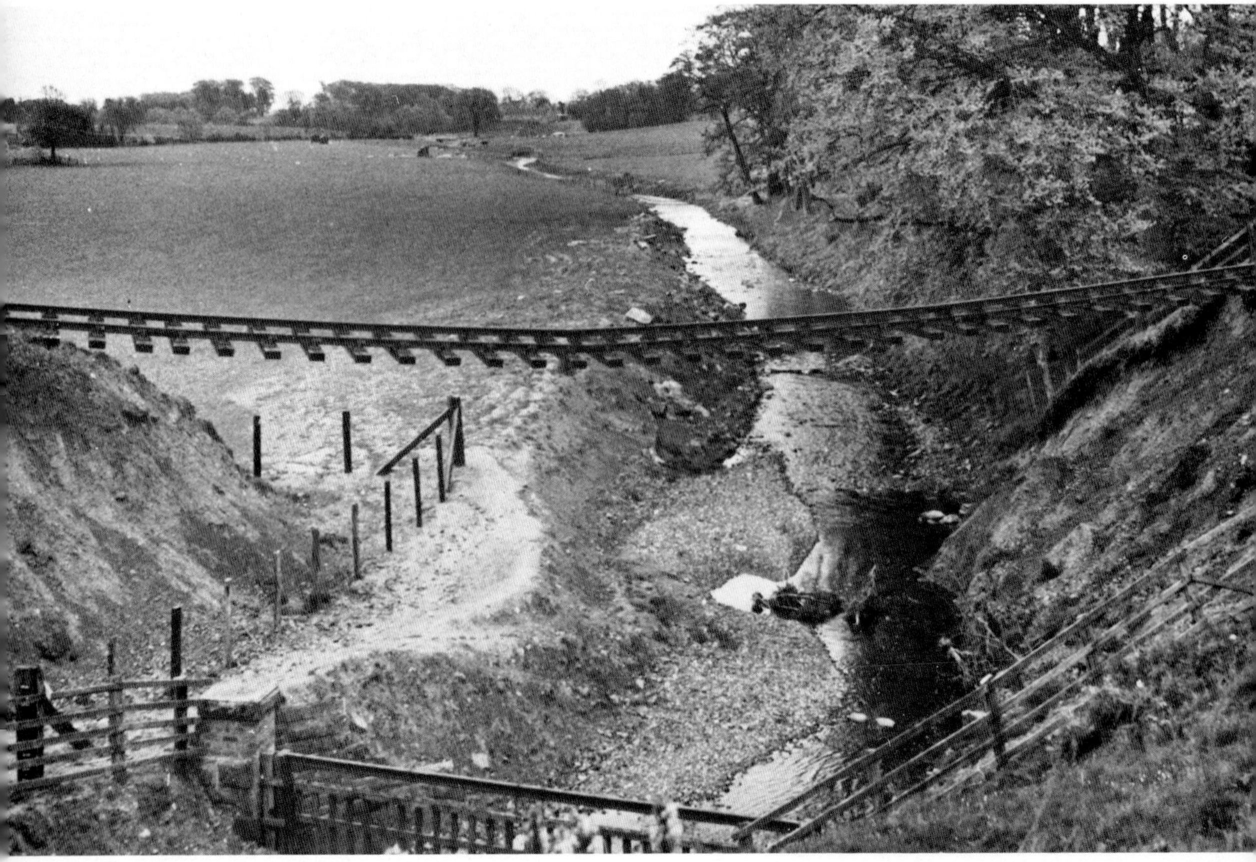

Above left: Class G5 0-4-4T No 67248 with a Duns-Berwick train on 3 August 1951, after restoration of the service between Duns and Berwick following repairs to the flood damage, but it lasted only until September 1951.
Locomotive Publishing Co/Ian Allan Library

Left: Langton Burn, to the west of Duns, showing the severe damage to the line inflicted by the East Coast floods in August 1948 (a photograph taken the following year).
W. A. Camwell

Above: Greenlaw station on 15 May 1958: Class J35/4 0-6-0 No 64494 with a pick-up freight. *W. S. Sellar*

Centre right: Earlston station on 29 May 1959: Class J36 0-6-0 No 65233 with a freight for St Boswells. *J. Spencer Gilks*

Right: A North British relic at Earlston in January 1965 — the parcels van had been in use as a store. *N. Caplan*

Above: The Leaderfoot viaduct near St Boswells was one of the outstanding examples of civil engineering in the Border Country: Class J35/4 0-6-0 No 64494 crossing with a freight for Greenlaw on 15 May 1958. *W. S. Sellar*

Below: Ravenswood junction on 29 May 1959, where the Berwickshire joined the Waverley Line. *J. Spencer Gilks*

Above: St Boswells engine shed on 12 June 1949 with Class J39/2 0-6-0 No 64877 and (background) J36 0-6-0 No 65242. *W. A. Camwell*

Below: The former engine shed as it was 15 years on in July 1964 with the typical North British water tank still in position. *N. Caplan*

These two photographs are not of the Berwickshire itself but they so help to bring home the tremendous destructive force of the 1948 floods and the scale of the engineering works needed to repair this damage:

Above: All that was left of Free Kirk bridge between Reston and Grantshouse: taken on 15 August 1948. *British Railways*

Below: Testing Free Kirk bridge on 24 December 1948 with the unique combination of Class A4 Pacific No 60012 *Commonwealth of Australia* and 'Hunt' Class D49/1 4-4-0 No 62706 *Forfarshire*. *British Railways*

The Eyemouth Branch

Only a 3-mile branch, but with the lovely coastline as background and the interesting little fishing port as terminus. It had a special charm and managed somehow to last until February 1962 in spite of economic change and the suspension of services for almost a year from August 1948 when its viaduct was damaged by the floods.

Above: Burnmouth station on 18 September 1950: Class J39/3 0-6-0 No 64843 waiting in the bay platform with a train for Eyemouth. *H. D. Bowtell*

Below: The same scene but it was nine years on — 11 August 1959 — and the engine was again No 64843. So many of the Border Country lines had the same engines working them for many years, especially before 1939. *R. E. Toop*

Above: Near Burnmouth on 24 August 1937: Class J21 0-6-0 LNER No 1562 with a train for Eyemouth.
Locomotive Publishing Co/Ian Allan Library

Below: Class D20 4-4-0 LNER No 2354 with an Eyemouth train near Burnmouth on 25 August 1947.
Locomotive Publishing Co/Ian Allan Library

Above: On the branch: Class J39/1 0-6-0 No 64941 with a train for Burnmouth on 10 July 1954. *J. Robertson*

Below: Leaving Eyemouth in style: Class J39/3 0-6-0 No 64843 with the 17.05 for Burnmouth on 19 August 1957. *W. J. V. Anderson*

Above: Eyemouth station on 21 June 1947: Class J25 0-6-0 LNER No 5039 with a train for Burnmouth.
W. A. Camwell

Below: The viaduct after one of the piers had collapsed during the East Coast floods of 12 August 1948.
The Scotsman

The Waverley Line

The Waverley was not of course a branch line, but it is unthinkable to exclude altogether from the album, the *Spine* route of the Border Country from which so many branches radiated. The Waverley attracted and held the interest and affection of railway enthusiasts to a degree far beyond its relatively modest significance as a trunk route between Scotland and England. Its course was through a countryside outstandingly rich in historical and romantic associations to which the Waverley can fairly be said to have added during its century of service to the Border Country community.

Even in that railway heyday of the summer of 1914, there were only eight trains daily between Edinburgh and Carlisle (including the Sleeper trains) and the only Sunday train was the 22.00 sleeper. There were however additional local trains between Edinburgh and Hawick

and Hawick and Carlisle. By the 1960s the service was indeed attenuated.

The Waverley has had an album to itself and has featured prominently in many books. This must serve as the excuse for the small coverage here — even if this must disappoint the devotees of the Waverley. The focus is upon the junction stations and freight traffic gets a fairer share than has sometimes been the case.

Below: At the northern end at Arniston: Class J27 0-6-0 No 64555 with a coal train on 5 September 1963. *D. Cross*

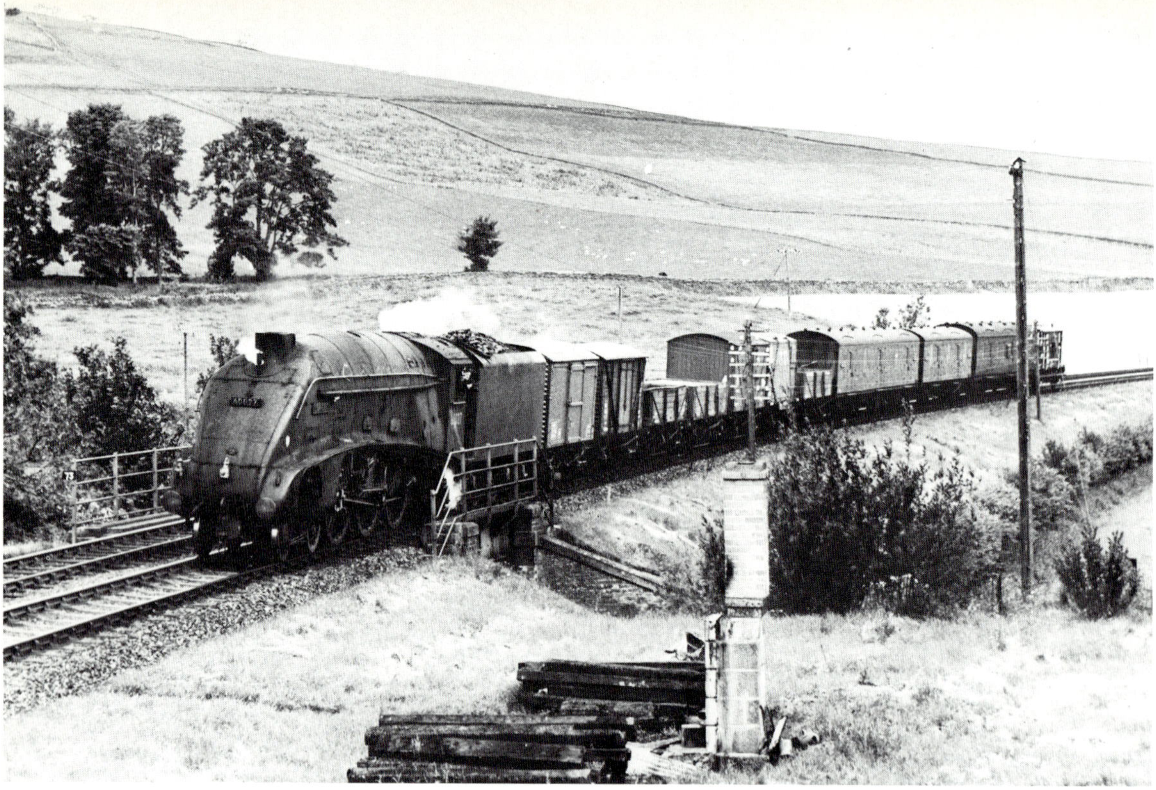

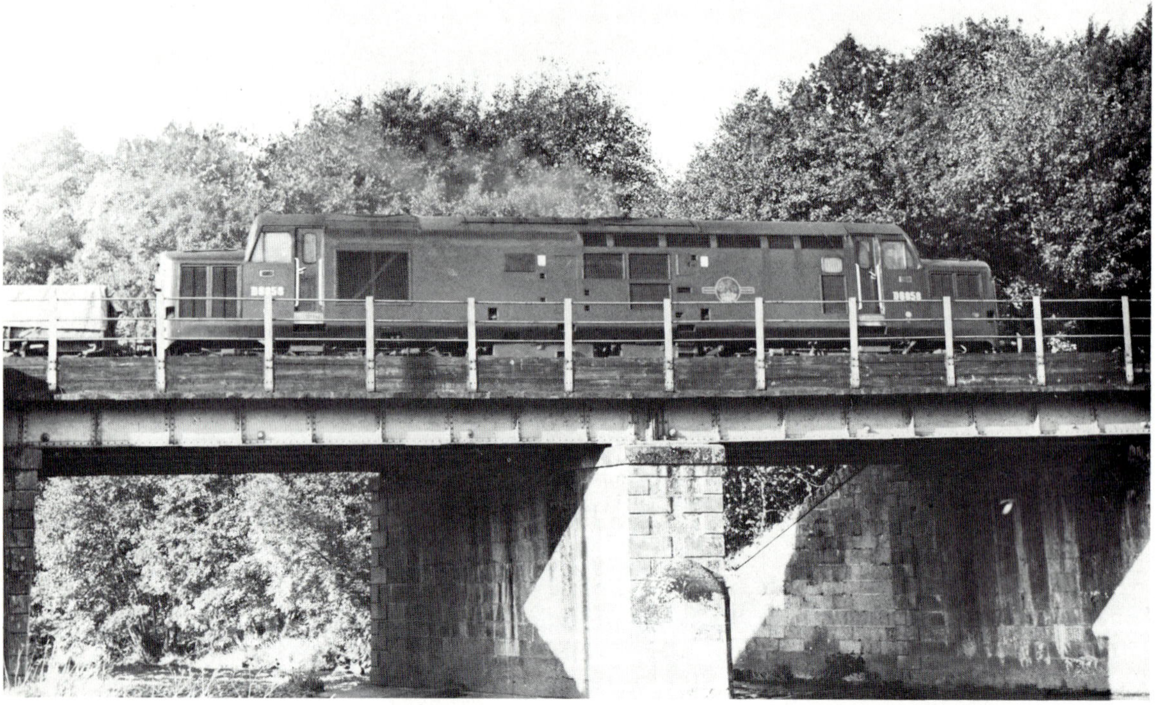

Left: A sorry come-down for a Gresley Pacific: Class A4 No 60027 *Merlin* heading a short freight train from Millerhill to Carlisle near Bowland on 8 July 1965.   *G. T. Robinson*

Below left: Crossing Gala Water near Bowland on 14 October 1968: English Electric Co-Co No D6858 with a freight for Millerhill.   *C. J. M. Lofthus*

Right: Heading north from Galashiels on 25 June 1966: Brush Co-Co No D1543 with a car/lorry freight. *C. J. M. Lofthus*

Below: Class B1 4-6-0 No 61354 leaving Galashiels on 20 July 1964 with the 16.10 Edinburgh-Hawick — in wonderfully fine condition for these closing years of 'steam'.   *G. Kinghorn*

Above: Galashiels station on 8 May 1950 and a busy morning scene: 'Hunt' Class D49/1 4-4-0 No 62715 *Ruxburghshire* with the 08.36 Edinburgh-Hawick stopping train and Class B1 4-6-0 No 61358 with the 07.57 from Edinburgh via Peebles. *W. A. Camwell*

Below: Very early days indeed at St Boswells — and all eyes are on the photographer! Note the minimal cab protection for the crew. *Ian Allan Library*

Above: North British days at St Boswells: Wheatley 2-4-0 No 1256. Note the typical North British carriages with their running boards. *Ian Allan Library*

Below: St Boswells South box in October 1963 — a good example of this type of North British box. Note the elegant bracket lamp in front. *N. Caplan*

Left: Class A3 Pacific No 60099 *Call Boy* with a part-fitted freight approaching St Boswells from the south at Kelso junction, where the Tweed Valley line from Berwick joined the Waverley Line — 1 August 1963. *N. Pollock*

Below: Hawick station early this century. A photograph which has captured so well the bustling atmosphere of a junction station when the railways dominated travel. *Ian Allan Library*

Right: Hawick station on 13 August 1955: 'Hunt' Class D49/2 4-4-0 No 62747 *The Percy* with the 16.32 for Newcastle via the Border Counties line. *I. S. Carr*

Below right: Near Borthwick on 29 August 1956: Class A1 Pacific No 60154 *Bon Accord* with the 22.35 Kings Cross-Edinburgh. The Royal Mail vans provide the clue — for this train had been diverted to the Waverley Line because of flood damage to the East Coast route. Often enough, it was the Waverley Line which came to the rescue when trouble hit the main line. *I. S. Pearsall*

73

Three scenes from LNER days on the Waverley Line, the first two taken near Hawick

Above: In 1932: the 'Northern Belle' with Class J39 0-6-0 LNER No 2736 piloting Class K2 2-6-0 with the J39 proudly displaying the distinguished headboard of the train. *R. B. Haddon*

Below: In 1927: 'Scott' Class D30/2 4-4-0 No 9412 *Laird O'Monkbarns* with the 15.15 Edinburgh-St Pancras. *R. B. Haddon*

Bottom: Leaving Stobs Camp in 1927: an Edinburgh-Silloth excursion headed by 'Intermediate' class 4-4-0 No 9889 and 'Scott' class 4-4-0 No 9412. This picture reminds one of the days when the North British Railway operated lines in Cumberland as well as in Northumberland. *R. B. Haddon*

Right: A glorious evocation of the stern challenge to the steam locomotive presented by the long, hard climb to Whitrope Summit: Class V2 2-6-2 No 60970 with a fitted freight on 8 July 1961. *P. Riley*

Left: Another V2 on Whitrope: No 60824 with a Carlisle-Millerhill freight on 8 July 1965. *G. T. Robinson*

Below left: At Whitrope summit in July 1961: Class B1 4-6-0 No 61178 with a southbound freight. *D. E. Esau*

Right: Whitrope siding box on 4 August 1964 — in all its bleak isolation. *N. Caplan*

Centre right: Whitrope — and bleaker still during that very hard winter of January 1963. Class J38 0-6-0 No 65914 with a team going in to lift snow. *W. S. Sellar*

Below: On the great sweeping curve of the southern approach to Riccarton Junction: Class V2 2-6-2 No 60836 with the South & West Railway Society's excursion from Euston to Aberdeen on 3 September 1966. *D. E. Gouldthorp*

Above left: Class A2 Pacific No 60529 *Pearl Diver* (inaptly named on this glacial day!) running into a wintry Riccarton Junction with a Niddrie-Kingmoor freight on 2 December 1961. *W. S. Sellar*

Below left: The grip of winter tightens on Riccarton Junction during that bitter January 1963: Class 4F 0-6-0 No 44081 together with Stanier '5' 4-6-0 No 45103 and Ivatt 2-6-0 No 43138 battling against heavy odds on snow clearance duty. *P. Brock*

Above: Near Steele Road — and so typical of the sweeping moorland of this part of the Waverley Line — Class V2 2-6-2 No 60927 with an Edinburgh-Carlisle train. *E. Treacy*

Below: At Carlisle Citadel on 20 August 1960: 'Glen' class 4-4-0 No 62488 *Glen Aladale* with the 12.20 (SO) from Hawick. *K. M. Falconer*

The Lauder Branch

The 10½-mile line from Fountainhall on the Waverley line climbed high up in the hills to Oxton and then kept close to Leader Water. It was an optimistic project to build such a branch and the passenger service was withdrawn as far back as September 1932. In 1910, the service had been only three trains in each direction on weekdays with an additional train on Saturdays. No photograph of the passenger service in operation has come to hand. The freight service lasted until final closure came in October 1958.

Above: Fountainhall: the Branch Line Society's 'Lauder Special' with Standard 2-6-0 No 78049 on 15 November 1958, after closure of the branch. *W. S. Sellar*

Below: Oxton station on 14 October 1954 — the only intermediate station. The branch freight was being worked by Class J67/1 0-6-0T No 68511 — one of the former Great Eastern Railway engines to Holden's design of 1890. *W. A. Camwell*

Above: Climbing to the summit on the return from Lauder on 14 October 1954. Note the tender fitted to No 68511 whose side tanks were empty with water being supplied from the tender. *W. A. Camwell*

Centre right: The very modest station at Lauder on 14 October 1954 with No 68511. *W. A. Camwell*

Below right: Lauder station as it was on 10 January 1965 — the end of the line in every sense. *N. Caplan*

The Selkirk Branch

The $6\frac{1}{4}$-mile branch from Galashiels served the County Town, and Selkirk in its heyday had many textile mills. For many years the passenger service was outstandingly good. In 1914, there were nine trains in each direction on weekdays with additional Saturday trains and the last train of the day from Galashiels departed for Selkirk as late as 23.15. In North British days, there were sidings for the Ettrick, Yarrow and St Mary's Mills. The passenger service was withdrawn in September 1958 and final closure came in 1965. Despite the relatively late withdrawal of the passenger service, it has proved difficult to obtain suitable photographs of this line.

Below: Lindean station on 4 April 1959: 'Glen' class 4-4-0 No 62471 *Glen Falloch* in impeccable condition with a special. *W. S. Sellar*

Right: Selkirk station and yard on 21 June 1947: 'Glen' Class D34 4-4-0 LNER No 2483 *Glen Garry* with the 19.55 to Galashiels. Mr Camwell has noted that the Selkirk branch had been worked formerly by railcars. *W. A. Camwell*

Below right: The good-looking station building at Selkirk in July 1964. *N. Caplan*

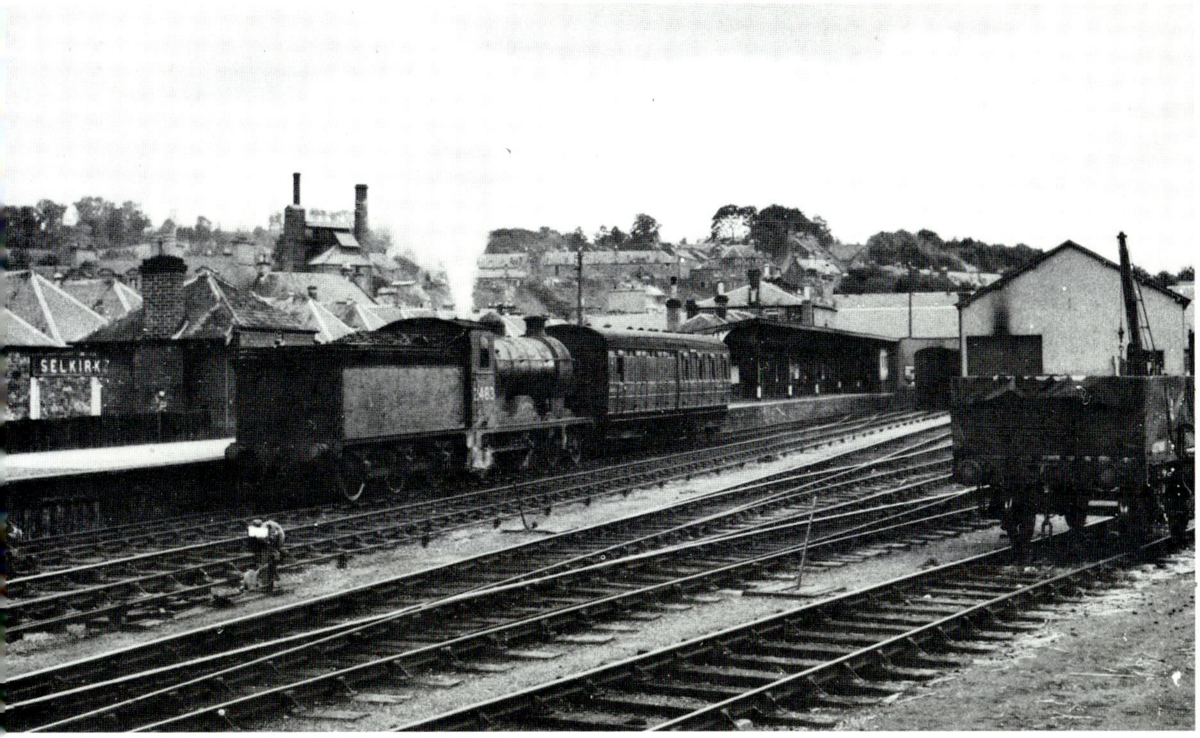
SELKIRK

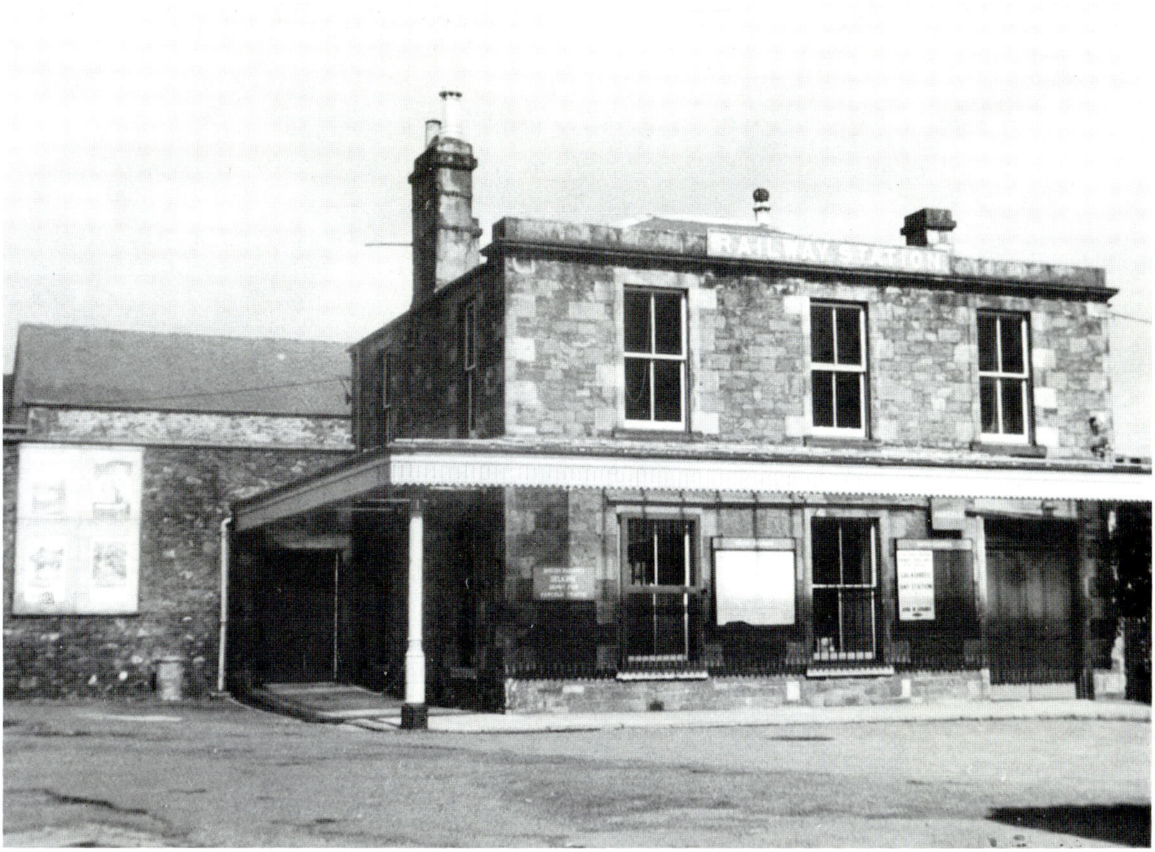
RAILWAY STATION

The Langholm Branch

The 7-mile line from Riddings junction on the Waverley line ran through the lovely Esk Valley and it had some fine viaducts. For most of its life, it had a good passenger service with through trains to and from Carlisle. It was another quiet rural line though the Glentarras Distillery had a siding for many years. The branch survived longer than most — it did not close until June 1964.

Above: Riddings junction: Class J35/4 0-6-0 No 64511 with a train for Langholm. *W. A. Camwell*

Below: The handsome Riddings viaduct over Liddel Water: Class J39/2 0-6-0 No 64877 crossing with the 10.06 Riddings-Langholm train in July 1961. *P. Brock*

Above right: Leaving Canonbie in August 1961: Fairburn 2-6-4T No 42081. *D. E. Esau*

Right: Near Gilnockie on 8 August 1962: Class J39/2 0-6-0 No 64895 with the 09.10 Langholm-Riddings. No 64895 was one of the last ex-LNER engines to work from the former North British shed at Carlisle Canal. *S. C. Crook*

Above left: Ivatt 2-6-0 No 43011 with an afternoon train for Carlisle near Gilnockie on 6 April 1964.
W. A. C. Smith

Below left: Another good viaduct on the branch: Tarrasfoot viaduct on 18 April 1964. The train engine was Ivatt 2-6-0 No 43045. *M. Dunnett*

The terminus at Langholm:

Above: On 4 August 1951: Class J36 0-6-0 No 65312 with a train from Carlisle. The J36 had been called on at Riddings to replace a failed J39. *H. D. Bowtell*

Below: Class J35/4 0-6-0 No 64511 with a train from Riddings and a freight train for Carlisle. *W. A. Camwell*

Leadburn to Peebles & Galashiels

The line from Edinburgh to Peebles was opened in July 1855 and the extension to Galashiels came much later on in October 1864 — 28 miles from Leadburn. The passenger service was quite good: in 1914, there were six trains on weekdays from Edinburgh through to Galashiels with an extra train on Saturdays as far as Peebles. There was one train on Sundays — the 16.00 which was allowed just under two hours for the 45½ miles from Edinburgh to Galashiels. By 1957, however, the service was down to three trains only with additional trains on Saturdays and the Sunday train had disappeared. The final phase of operation of the line was by dmus. The line was closed entirely in February 1962.

It is interesting to note that although there was a junction connection with the Caledonian Railway's Peebles branch at Peebles, the lack of co-operation between the two companies made it impossible for people from Galashiels to reach Glasgow via Symington which could have been a fast journey, because the North British arrivals at Peebles were timed for 10 minutes *after* the departures by the Caledonian for Symington!

Above: Leadburn station on 3 February 1962: Class J37 0-6-0 No 64587 with the Stephenson Locomotive Society's 'Farewell to Peebles' special which was run from Edinburgh on the eve of closure of the line.
W. A. C. Smith

NORTH BRITISH STATION, PEEBLES.

Above: Peebles station early this century with a Wheatley 2-4-0 about to leave for Galashiels. This picture brings out so well the high standards of the railways in late Victorian and Edwardian times — a scrupulously clean station, the bank properly kept and the hanging flower baskets (the Peebles district has always had good gardeners). *H. C. Casserley collection*

Below: The same station some 60 years on — and a sorry contrast. The 14.06 Galashiels-Edinburgh formed by 2-car dmu on 11 November 1961. *W. A. C. Smith*

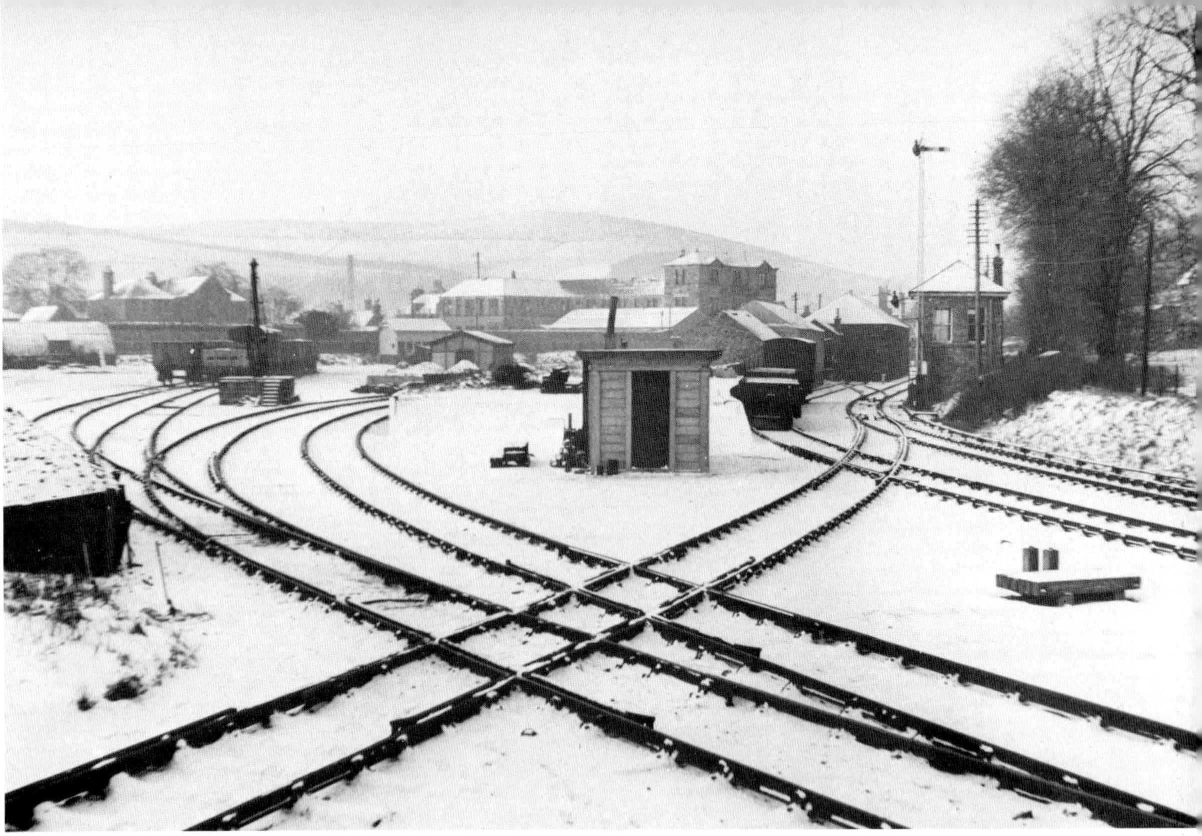

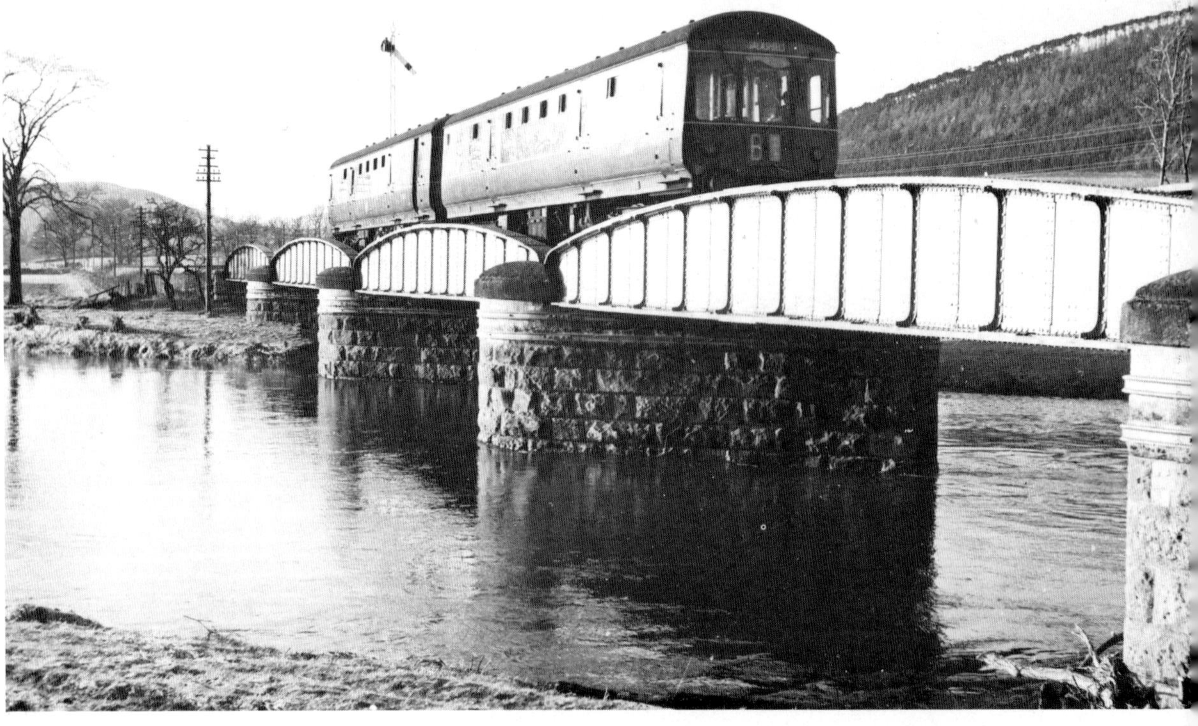

Left: The south end of Peebles station in November 1961 showing the yard and the junction connection with the Caledonian branch curving away sharply to the left. *D. C. Smith*

Below left: Crossing the Tweed at Cardrona on 20 January 1962 — 2-car dmu forming the 13.18 Edinburgh-Galashiels. *W. A. C. Smith*

Above: Innerleithen station on 11 November 1961 with 2-car dmu forming the 14.06 Galashiels-Edinburgh. Note the unusual 'cantilevered' signalbox — and the trimly-kept platforms even though closure was only weeks away. *W. A. C. Smith*

Centre right: Innerleithen station in September 1964, looking east. *N. Caplan*

Below right: Walkerburn station on 11 November 1961, looking east. *W. A. C. Smith*

Left: Class B1 4-6-0 No 61355 with an afternoon train to Edinburgh via Peebles soon after leaving Galashiels on 1 August 1953. *P. B. Whitehouse*

Above: Galashiels shed on 19 June 1949: in the foreground, 'Glen' class 4-4-0 No 62471 *Glen Falloch* and behind former Great Eastern Railway Class J67/1 0-6-0T No 68511, tender-fitted for water supply (the ex-GER tank engines worked the Lauder branch freights). *W. A. Camwell*

Below: Galashiels shed on 28 April 1952 with another of the ex-GER 0-6-0T engines — Class J69/1 No 68492 with fitted-tender. *H. C. Casserley*

Leadburn to Dolphinton

The 10-mile branch was opened in July 1864 and it was closed entirely in April 1933 in the wake of the economic depression which caused so many branch line closures during 1931-35. Not surprisingly, it was a line which escaped the attention of all but a very few photographers. Happily, Mr E. Jefferies of West Linton has come to my aid here with very interesting photographs and information about the railwaymen working the branch.

Writing about the line in 1955, H. A. Vallance noted: 'Traffic was never heavy. What might have been quite an attractive cross-country route, at least for tourists, was marred by poor connections at Dolphinton, where each company had its own station, although there was direct physical connection between the two railways.' The uneasy relations between the North British and the Caledonian Railways certainly militated against the development of a cross-country route. If, in 1914, the intrepid traveller had set out to get from Leadburn to the Caledonian main line at Carstairs by the afternoon train, he would have had to wait at Dolphinton for one and a half hours for his 'connection'. Travelling in the morning, his wait would have been four hours!

Below: Leadburn station in December 1963 after closure of the line to Peebles — the bay platform for Dolphinton to the left. *N. Caplan*

Above: Broomlee station circa 1895 with the station staff and train crew posing happily for their picture on the level crossing! They included: Joe Joss, stationmaster; Andrew Simpson, guard; Tom Cowie, station clerk; Peter Luckly, driver and John Fleming, signalman. The train was a freight from Dolphinton with (probably) a Holmes 0-6-0 North British No 781. *E. Jefferies collection*

Centre right: Dolphinton station on 25 March 1933: Class C15 4-4-2T LNER No 9043 with a train from Leadburn. No 9043 was the most regular engine on the branch, with No 9048 as an occasional replacement sent up by St Margarets shed. *A. Aitken*

Bottom right: In close-up: the two sets of trainmen who worked the branch during the week before closure. From left to right: Andrew Simpson, guard (some 40 years on from the picture above); a relief fireman; Bob Scobie, driver; John Dobson, driver; Bob Fell, fireman and Jack Hutchinson, guard. *A. Aitken*

Above: Dolphinton station with No 9048 waiting to leave for Leadburn. *R. Brown*

Below: The end of the branch: the last passenger train at Broomlee on 31 March 1933 with No 9043 and a 'crowd' of passengers with the stationmaster, George Greig. *E. Jefferies collection*

Carstairs to Dolphinton

The Caledonian Railway's 11-mile branch to Dolphinton proved to be a dead end line even if it perhaps helped to check a move by the North British westward from its own branch to Dolphinton. The passenger service was always poor — as noted above in the context of the North British branch. But it survived somehow until November 1950 and so it is rather surprising that only one photograph of the line in operation has come to hand. This justifies including a few illustrations of the Carstairs junction end.

Above: Dolphinton junction: the branch was to the left of the box. Stanier '5' 4-6-0 No 44925 with the 15.10 Carstairs-Edinburgh.
W. A. C. Smith

Left: Dolphinton station on 10 September 1932: Midland Compound 4-4-0 No 917 with a train for Carstairs. An impressive engine for the one coach train, but No 917 was stabled at Dalry Road shed and it occasionally worked the branch when idle for a few hours at Carstairs.
A. Aitken

Top: Dolphinton station on 28 July 1963 — well-converted to a home. *N. Caplan*

Above: A reminder of the Caledonian years at Carstairs: withdrawn Pickersgill 4-4-0s Nos 54463 and 54502 on 29 July 1963. *N. Caplan*

Right: The impressive coaling tower of Carstairs shed with Stanier '5' 4-6-0 No 45245 on 29 July 1963. It is so difficult now to realise that these so-familiar features of the major sheds are no more. *N. Caplan*

Symington to Peebles

The Caledonian Extension Railway had been planned to construct a branch from Symington to Peebles as early as 1846. But its Bill failed in Parliament in the face of the opposition by the North British Railway. The scheme was revived in part in 1858 when the Symington, Biggar & Broughton Railway was authorised to build the 8-mile line to Broughton and this was completed in 1860. The further 11 miles on to Peebles were opened in 1864. From the start, the branch was worked by the Caledonian which absorbed the local company in 1861. The passenger service survived until June 1950, but freight workings continued for many years, principally to serve the meat plant at Broughton.

Above: Symington station on 19 June 1965 — the branch to Peebles curving away to the left (the station was later demolished entirely). *N. Caplan*

Below: Symington station on 9 June 1949: Class 4P 4-4-0 No 40903 (ex-LMS 3 cylinder compound) with the 12.08 Symington-Peebles *W. A. Camwell*

Above left: Crossing the Clyde near Coulter on 2 May 1962: Stanier '5' 4-6-0 No 45161 with a Broughton-Symington freight. *W. S. Sellar*

Left: Biggar station on 2 January 1965. *N. Caplan.*

Above: Hughes/Fowler 'Crab' 2-6-0 No 42737 between Biggar and Broughton with a special on 19 March 1964 — the train had been shortened to three coaches only for 'rounding' at Broughton. *D. C. Smith*

Centre right: The special approaching Broughton. *W. J. V. Anderson*

Below right: Broughton station on 2 May 1962: Stanier '5' 4-6-0 No 45161 with the branch freight. *W. S. Sellar*

Above: Lyne station on 20 June 1964 after its skilful conversion to a home. *N. Caplan*

Three scenes at Peebles station:

Below: On 1 August 1931: McIntosh 0-6-0 No 17440 with a train for Symington. *H. C. Casserley*

Above: On 9 June 1949: Class 4P 4-4-0 No 40903 with the
13.50 for Symington. *W. A. Camwell*

Below: Pickersgill '3P' 4-4-0 No 54477 with a train for
Symington. *J. L. Stevenson*

The Wanlockhead Branch

It is a matter of great regret that the 7¼-mile branch from Elvanfoot on the Caledonian main line to Leadhills and Wanlockhead was overlooked by railway photographers during its short life because pictures of the line in operation are scarce. It was indeed a branch of special interest which was brought into being to serve the long-established lead mines of the district. It was opened in two sections: from Elvanfoot to Leadhills in October 1901, and then on to Wanlockhead in October 1902. In 1910, there were three trains in each direction on weekdays; the service in the 1930s was four trips daily by the Sentinel steam railcar with two freight workings weekly.

During its so-brief life of 37 years, the branch had the distinction of the highest summit level in Great Britain worked by standard gauge adhesion: 1,498ft compared with the 1,484ft of the Highland Railway's summit at Druimuachdar. Thanks to the courtesy of Mr H. C.

Casserley, there are here some photographs of trains working the line in 1931. The line was closed entirely in January 1939 — now it has been closed for longer than it was in operation!

At the Elvanfoot end:

Above: Elvanfoot station on 2 July 1964 with its fine setting of the Lowthers. *N. Caplan*

Above right: Stanier '5' 4-6-0 No 45029 leaving Elvanfoot with a southbound freight on 10 April 1965. *N. Caplan*

Right: The former junction of the Wanlockhead branch at Elvanfoot. *N. Caplan*

Above: Above Elvanfoot: showing the course of the former branch as it was in July 1964. *N. Caplan*

Left: The fine viaduct near Leadhills in July 1964 — 25 years after closure of the line. *N. Caplan*

Above right: Leadhills in the early years of the branch: Drummond 0-4-4T with a train which provided compartments for first class passengers. Note the solid bogie wheels of the engine. *Ian Allan Library*

Right: Leadhills station on 30 July 1931 with the 'name-board' picked out in pebbles on the right — a characteristic feature of many Scottish stations. Note also the similar advertisement for: 'Cheap Tickets are issued to Glasgow, Edinburgh, Moffat' and the catch points. *H. C. Casserley*

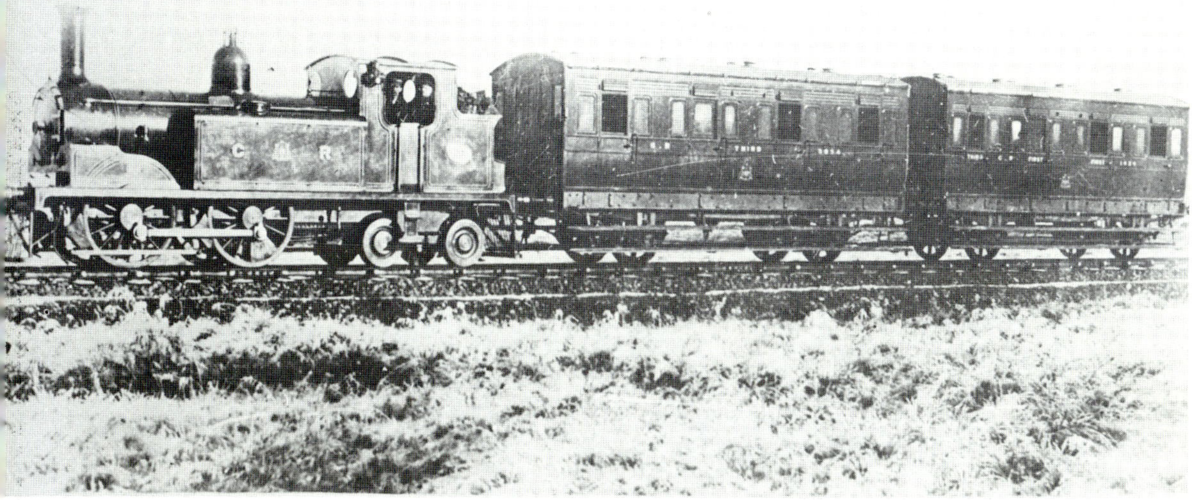

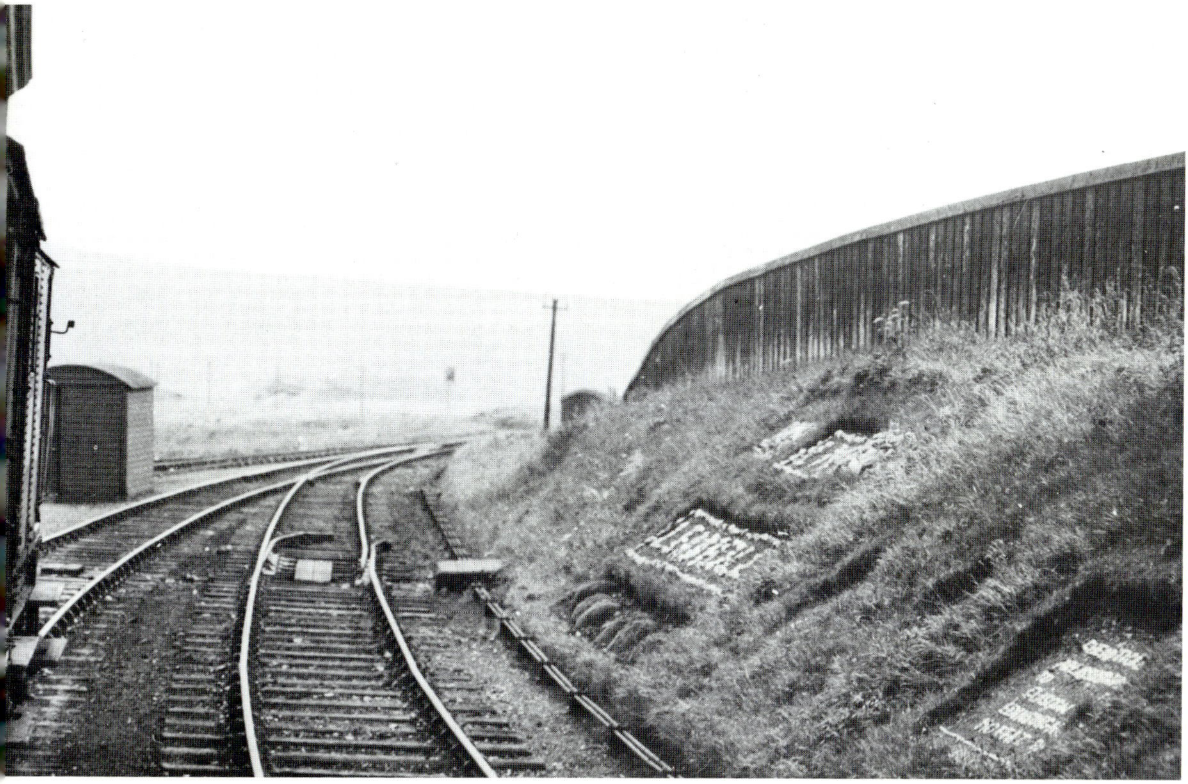

Above: The rugged approach to Wanlockhead — the former trackbed in April 1965. *N. Caplan*

Left: Wanlockhead station on 30 July 1931: McIntosh 0-4-4T LMS No 15181 shunting. *H. C. Casserley*

Bottom left: Wanlockhead — the same day, with No 15181 on a mixed train. *H. C. Casserley*

The Moffat Branch

This was a 'minnow' of a branch — just two miles from Beattock on the Caledonian main line. Moffat must have gained from the fact that railwaymen working at Beattock and on the famous Bank lived there because it had a service of 13 trains in each direction on weekdays in 1910. The passenger service was withdrawn in December 1954, though there continued to be a Saturdays only train for railway staff and their families. The freight service continued until final closure of the branch in April 1964. The little branch was dominated by Beattock and the bank which demand a few illustrations here.

Above: Beattock station on 7 May 1949: No 46656 with a train for Moffat. *J. L. Stevenson*

Below: Beattock shed on 3 August 1965 with Fairburn 2-6-4T No 42129 — the Moffat branch to the far right *N. Caplan*

MOFFAT
GENTLEMEN
£1000
SUNLIGHT
GUARANTEE OF PURITY

42192
Esso

Above left: Moffat station on 1 August 1931 with ex-LNWR railmotor train No 10657. The LMS treated the railmotors as coaching stock for numbering purposes. *H. C. Casserley*

Above: Moffat station on 3 August 1965 by when most of the buildings had been demolished. *N. Caplan*

Left: Thirty years on at Moffat: Fairburn 2-6-4T No 42192 with the daily freight on 3 April 1961. *A. Tyson*

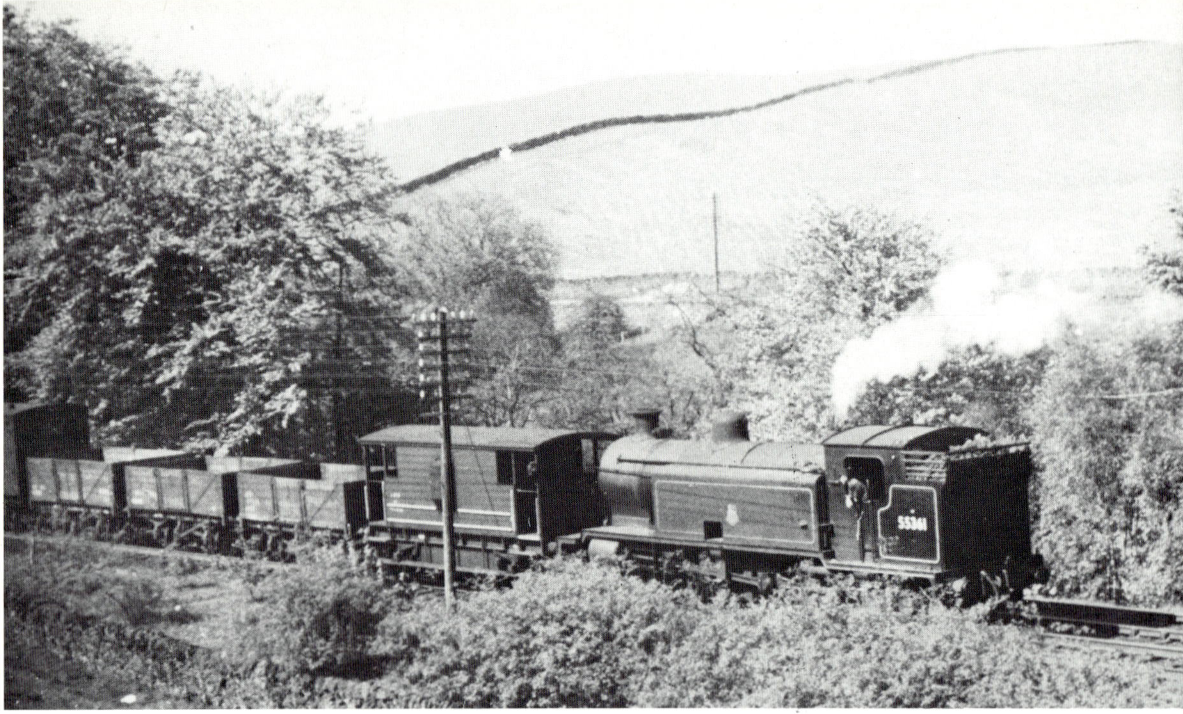
55361

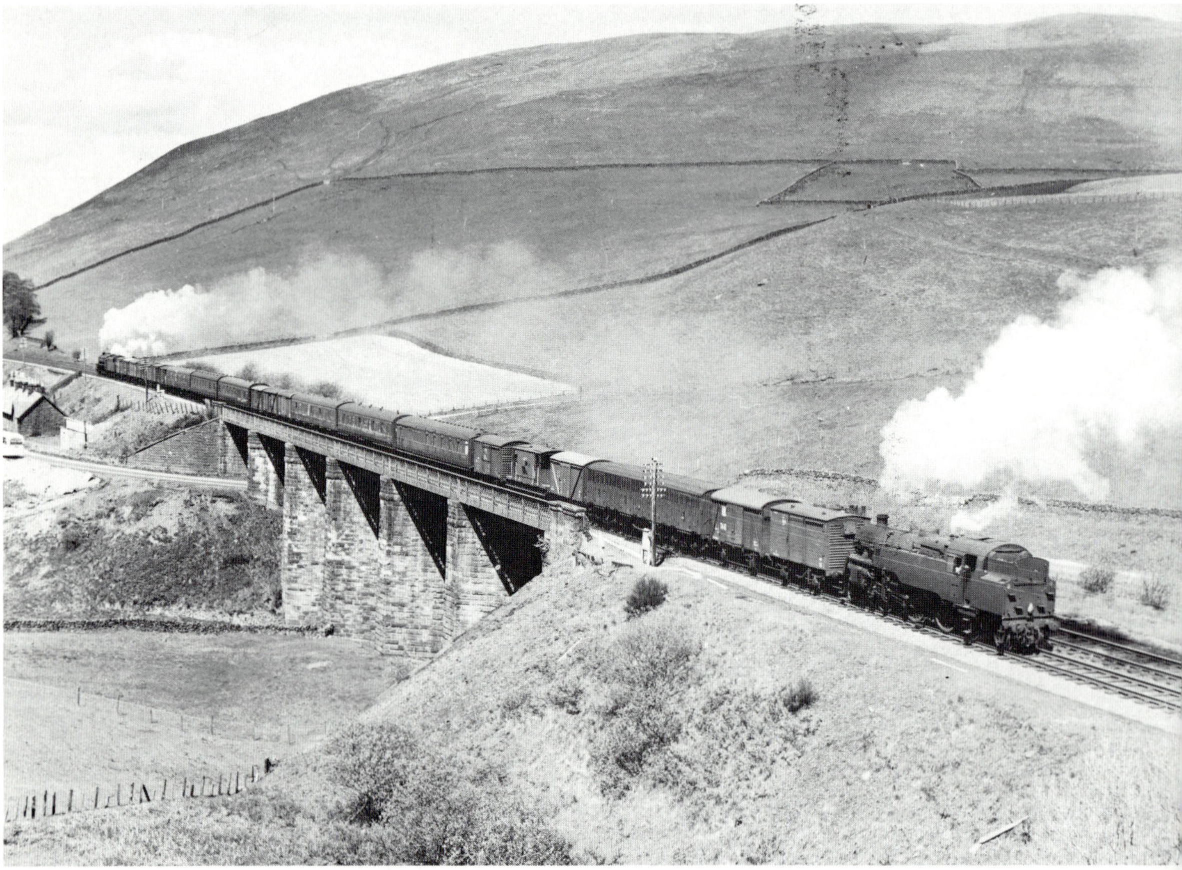

Left: Banking duty for No 55361 on 1 June 1951.
H. C. Casserley

Below left: At Harthope on the bank on 23 May 1965:
Standard 2-6-4T No 80002 banking a Carlisle-Perth
parcels train; the train engine was Stanier '5' 4-6-0
No 45066. *D. Cross*

Above: Class 4F 0-6-0 No 44326 with a railway staff
special at Beattock summit on 26 July 1952. *J. Robertson*

Below: Beattock summit box on 10 April 1965: 1,015ft
above sea level. Note the water column — once so
necessary for replenishment after the hard slog to the
summit. *N. Caplan*

Newcastle & Carlisle Railway

The 60¼-mile line linking the East and West Coast main lines formed the southward boundary of the Border Country in railway terms. It was completed as early as 1839 and it has survived all changes in the railway world to be able to welcome to its tracks the High Speed Trains when diverted from the East Coast, as these were in 1979 when Penmanshiel tunnel was blocked and under major repair.

The line has recently had a book to itself and so is featured here principally for its junctions with the branches covered in the album.

Above: Crossing the Tyne over Wylam bridge: Class B1 4-6-0 No 61219 with a Newcastle-Carlisle train on 12 April 1952. *J. W. Armstrong*

Left: The gantry signalbox of Hexham East with the remains of Hexham shed behind. *Ian Allan Library*

Above right: A survivor of Worsdell's 1886 design for the North Eastern Railway: Class J21 0-6-0 No 65070 at Hexham on 29 August 1956. *I. S. Carr*

Right: Hexham station on 12 November 1966: The 'Waverley' special of the A4 Preservation Society pausing for the 'A4' engine to take water. The water column and the water tank were such familiar features of the station scene in steam days and they ought not to be forgotten. *L. A. Nixon*

Above: The classic Pacific engine: Class A4 LNER No 4498 *Sir Nigel Gresley* (appropriately) with an excursion from Newcastle to Carlisle near Haltwhistle on 17 June 1972. *L. A. Nixon*

Below: Haltwhistle station on 12 April 1952: Class B1 4-6-0 No 61014 *Oribi* arriving with a Newcastle-Carlisle train. *J. W. Armstrong*

Above: Haltwhistle station early this century. Note the viaduct over the South Tyne — background, right — which carried the Alston branch. *H. C. Casserley collection*

Below: Haltwhistle station on 19 February 1972: the diesel multiple-units have taken over with a 4-car train for Newcastle and a 2-car train for Alston. *D. Cross*

Above: Brampton junction in 1952: Class B1 4-6-0
No 61276 arriving with a Carlisle-Newcastle train.
J. W. Armstrong

Left: Between Carlisle and Haltwhistle: Ivatt 2-6-0
No 43121 working hard with a SLS/BLS rail tour special
for the Alston branch on 26 March 1967. *D. E. Gouldthorp*

Below: Class V2 2-6-2 No 60964 passing How Mill on
27 July 1963 with the midday Stranraer-Newcastle Irish
boat train. *P. J. Robinson*

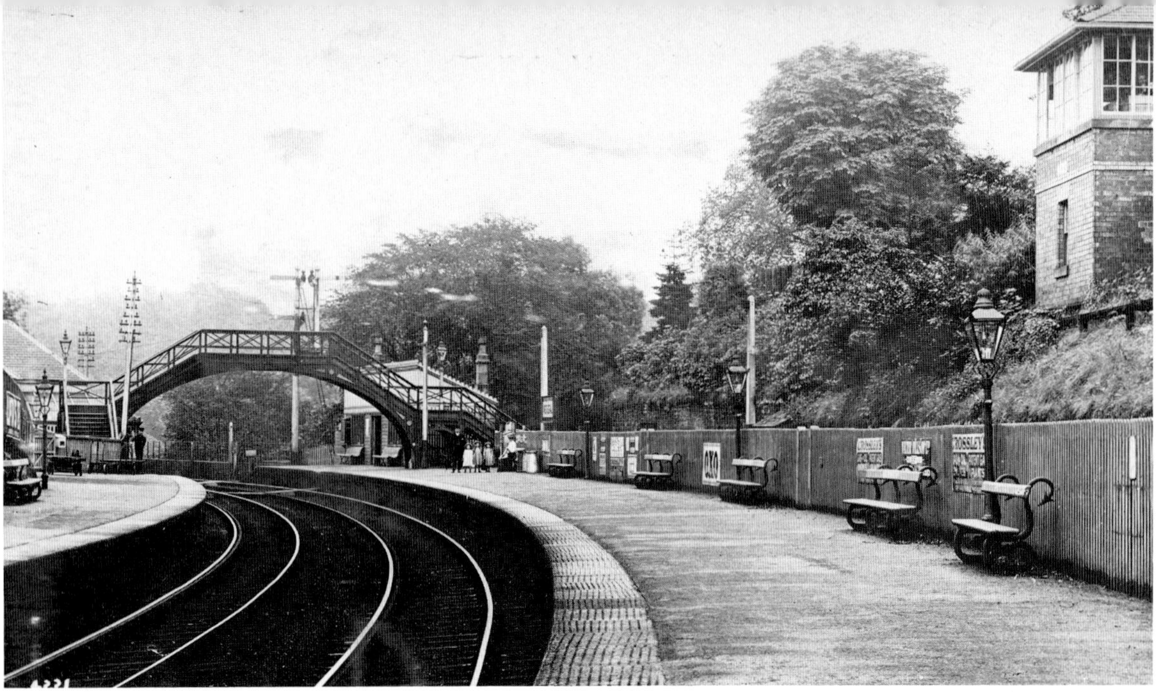
OXO
CROSSLEY

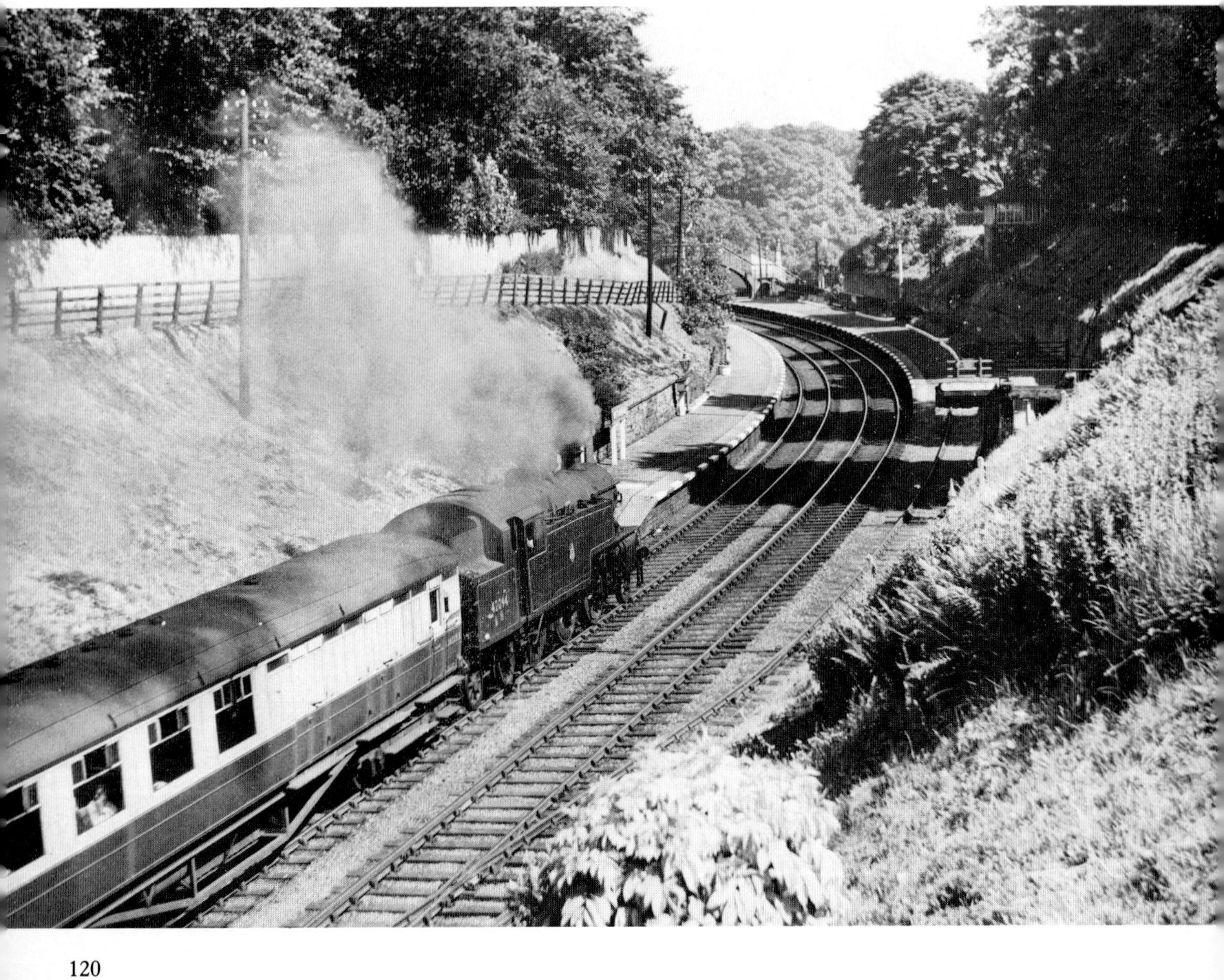

Left: Wetheral station early this century. Note the siting of the signalbox on the bank to improve visibility over the very sharp curve of the line.
Locomotive Publishing Co/Ian Allan Library

Below left: Wetheral station on 16 July 1955: Fairburn 2-6-4T No 42094 arriving with the 14.30 (SO) Carlisle-Newcastle train. *R. H. Leslie*

Right: Class K1 2-6-0 No 62027 crossing Wetheral viaduct with a Blaydon-Carlisle coal train on 5 November 1955. *R. H. Leslie*

Centre right: East of Scotby: Class K1 2-6-0 No 62030 with a Carlisle-Blaydon freight on 18 February 1956. *R. H. Leslie*

Below: The inevitability of change: HST Inter City 125 working as the 07.57 Edinburgh-Kings Cross and taking the Newcastle line out of Carlisle on 16 August 1979 (rear view). This was a diversion caused by the repair work on the Penmanshiel tunnel on the East Coast main line. *I. S. Carr*

The Allendale Branch

It was again lead mining which prompted the construction of this Border Country branch. The $13\frac{1}{2}$-mile line from Hexham climbed high up into the Northumberland fells and it had a rugged character of its own. The passenger service was withdrawn 50 years ago — in September 1930 — and it had always been infrequent. Even in 1914, there were only three trains in each direction on weekdays with additional trains on Mondays, Tuesdays and Saturdays. The freight service survived until final closure came in November 1950. Photographs of the line in operation are scarce.

Top left: The branch near its junction with the Newcastle & Carlisle line at Hexham — August 1950. *J. W. Armstrong*

Centre left: Class J21 0-6-0 No 65082 with the branch freight near Langley in 1950. *E. E. Smith*

Bottom left: Allendale station in August 1950: Riddles MoS, LNER Class J94, 0-6-0ST No 68059 with the branch freight. *J. W. Armstrong*

The Alston Branch

For the Border Country, this was an early branch line, for the 13½-mile line from Haltwhistle was opened in 1852. As it survived until 1976, it also proved to be the longest-lived of them all. This was always an interesting line with good viaducts on the long climb up to 905ft at Alston. The branch often knew the problems of working under severe winter conditions. There was a substantial freight traffic in coal mining days. The passenger service was limited for even in 1914 there were only four trains daily with an extra train on Saturdays, but — unusually — there were then morning and evening trains in each direction on Sundays.

Above: Haltwhistle station on 30 March 1957: Standard 2-6-0 No 77014 with the 11.50 for Alston. *I. S. Carr*

Below: Class J39/1 0-6-0 No 64814 crossing the South Tyne viaduct with the 17.40 Haltwhistle-Alston on 22 June 1957. *R. H. Leslie*

Above: Two-car dmu working the 17.34 Haltwhistle-Alston on 26 August 1970. *I. S. Carr*

Below: The fine Lambley viaduct: 8-car dmu 'Alstonian' special of the Wirral Railway Circle crossing en route for Alston on 15 April 1974. *I. S. Carr*

Above: Lambley station in November 1956: Class J39/1 0-6-0 No 64814 leaving for Alston. Note the tracks of the Lambley Colliery line to the left, centre. Once there was a 'mineral' line link between Lambley and Brampton Junction by the colliery branches. *J. W. Armstrong*

Below: The panorama of Lambley viaduct and station: Ivatt 2-6-0 No 43121 with SLS/BLS rail tour special on 26 March 1967. Note that the tracks of the line to Lambley Colliery had been lifted. *D. E. Gouldthorp*

Above: Alston station and box on 5 September 1955. *H. C. Casserley*

Left: Class J39/2 0-6-0 No 64842 with the 12.25 from Haltwhistle at Alston on 4 August 1956. *L. A. Strudwick*

Right: Alston station on 26 October 1970: 2-car dmu about to leave for Haltwhistle. Note the nice touch of the station gable finials!. *I. S. Carr*

The Brampton Town Branch

The little 1¼-mile line from Brampton junction on the Newcastle & Carlisle Railway had the unhappy distinction of being the first of Border Country branches to be closed. The passenger service was withdrawn at the end of October 1923 and the branch was closed entirely from 1 January 1924. Yet, before the motor car and bus took people away from the railway, Brampton had as many as 18 trains in each direction on weekdays. Pictures of the branch in action are scarce.

Above: Brampton junction station, early this century. *Locomotive Publishing Co/Ian Allan Library*

Below: Brampton Town station: Class BTP 0-4-4T No 1089 with a passenger train (probably circa 1920). Mr W. B. Yeadon has kindly provided details about this particular example of Fletcher's bogie tank passenger class built over the period 1874 to 1883: No 1089 was withdrawn on 12 April 1921, after being shedded at Carlisle (London Road). This engine was re-boilered with the boiler taken from 0-6-0 class '1001' No 1216, which explains the unusually close positioning of the dome to the chimney. Note also the typical North Eastern non-corridor third class brake with clerestory roof which was used so widely for local services. *W. B. Yeadon collection*

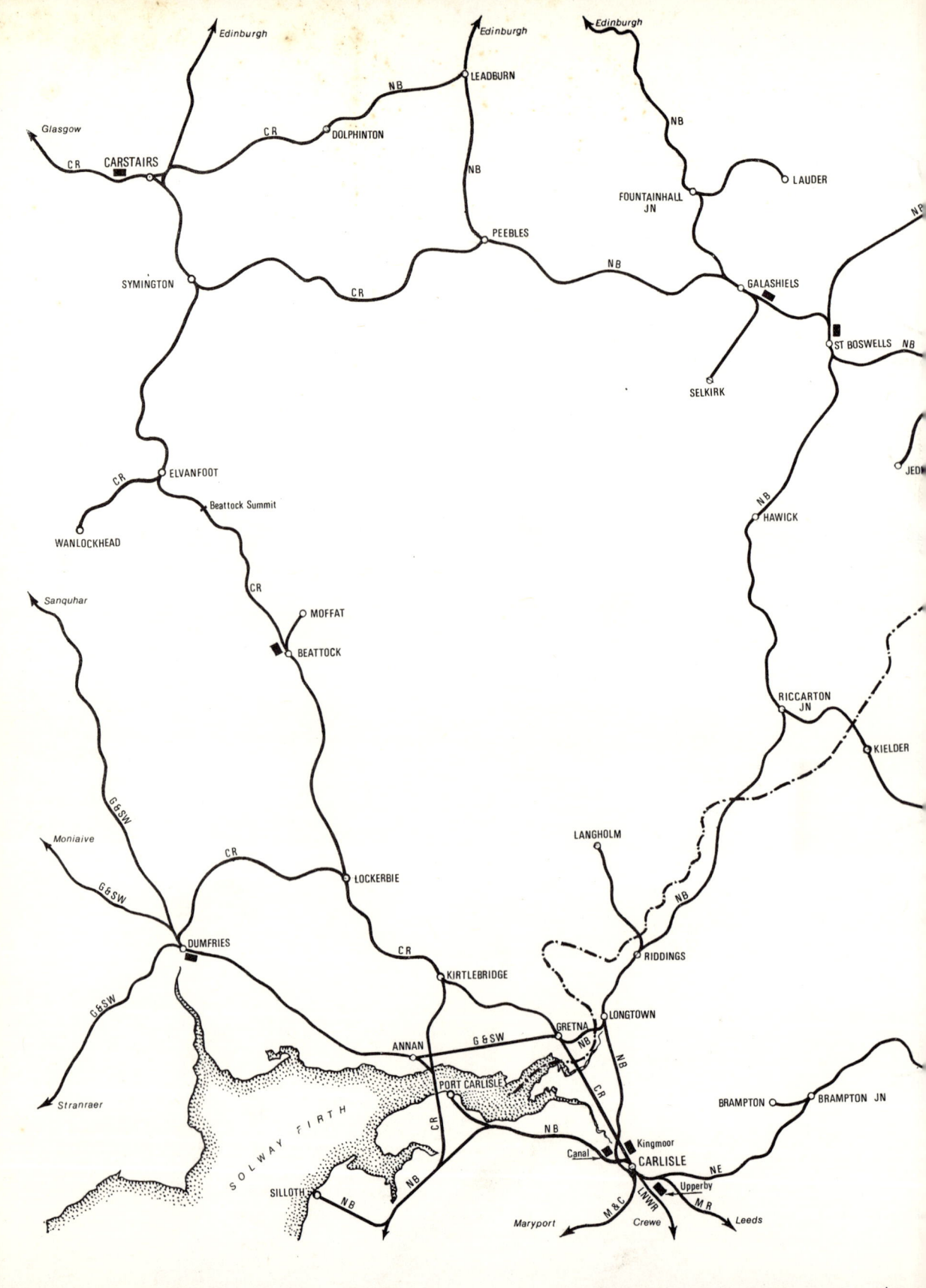